Dear Mike
We'll always thinking of you.
Thanks for your close friendship.
Sincerely
Rabbi X.
Laufer

Think Jewish

A Contemporary View of Judaism
A Jewish View of Today's World

Zalman I. Posner

KESHER PRESS
NASHVILLE, TENNESSEE

Other Works:

Reflections on the Sedra

Translations:

Tanya, Part III
Tanya, Part V
On the Teachings of Chassidus
On Learning Chassidus
The Tzemach Tzedek and the Haskala Movement
Kuntres Uma'ayan
Saying Tehillim

Library of Congress card number 78–71323

ISBN 0–9602394–0–5 Clothbound
ISBN 0–96–02394–1–3 Paperback

First printing March 1979
Second printing November 1979

Printed in the United States of America

My wife and I dedicate this volume
to our parents

Rabbi and Mrs. Sholom Posner

Rabbi and Mrs. Shlomo Aharon Kazarnovsky

who live lives to inspire their children.

May they be blessed with years of health and nachas from
"children and children's children occupied with the study of
Torah and the observance of mitzvos."

Foreword

What can a 35 century old tradition tell the 20th century?

The given American Jew is certainly a college graduate, probably with several years of graduate school as well. Too often Jewish education, whatever meager ration it was, probably ended before adolescence. When Jewishness and the ideas of the secular world conflict, in effect one is pitting a child against a sophisticated adult's conceptions. Considering the unequal match, it is no surprise that the secular view is often more persuasive, and the young Jew dismisses Judaism without even really encountering it.

This book endeavors to bridge that huge gap between the Jewish knowledge and the academic, to demonstrate that Judaism's teachings must be examined with the care and rigor one examines, say, political or economic or social or scientific offerings. Torah addresses the contemporary world, not necessarily agreeing with what is current by any means, but giving guidance and challenge and goals worthy of a thinking person. Today's world has not yet solved all its problems and shows little promise of solving many of them. Torah insights can add perspective badly needed.

The author has been privileged to address countless gatherings of Jewish students and has regularly participated in the "Encounter With Chabad," where scores of students experience Chassidic life in the Chabad community in Brooklyn. He draws on Chassidic sources and orientation in an endeavor to contribute the Chassidic perspective to the subjects at hand, though citations are seldom directly made.

The bulk of the essays in this book are based on questions these students posed. Some of these essays have appeared in *Challenge*, (London 1970), *A Woman of Valour* (London 1976) and in the journals *Yiddishe Heim* and *Ufaratzto*.

These essays are not necessarily sequential, and there is some recurrence of themes. Certain illustrations may be dated, e.g. "flower children"—but more current ones may readily be substituted. Today's contemporary example is tomorrow's anachronism.

In every stage of the development of this book my wife, Risia, was an unfailing source of encouragement and counsel. Her standards of clear thinking and expression were immeasurably valuable.

Nashville, Tennessee
20 Cheshvan 5739
November 20, 1978

Contents

What Is Chassidus?
What Is Chabad?

The history of Israel may be described as the unfolding
of Torah, its flowering, as conditions of life presented fresh
challenges calling for fresh responses. From within the
implicit of Torah, our Sages constantly articulated the answers to unprecedented problems. The seed contains
within it, in potentia, the massive growth of the oak; Torah
contains within its words all the verbalizations and exposi-
tions of the generations, the immense libraries of Torah
thought.

At one time, we may presume, a word was sufficient.
"Love your fellow as yourself" was all the admonition
needed to correct an erring person. But this idyllic state
didn't last long. Isaiah's and Amoses and the other
prophets had to spell it out more clearly and directly. Quit
abusing widows and orphans. Quit taking bribes, you
judges. The stirring cries of the prophets were extensions
of *Chumash,* verbalizations of the implicit.

As more generations passed, as the era of prophecy
ended with its direct G-d-man communication, the era of
the scholar opened, with its intellectual demands and standards. *Mishna* was produced. Its contemporaries did not
refer directly to *Chumash* for *Halacha* guidance but could
use the *Mishna.* A later generation needed the *Gemara's*
exposition to make *Mishna* intelligible, but the *Gemara*
again was a verbalization and extension of the implicit
within *Mishna.*

The great Codes and commentaries, Rambam and *Tur,*
Rashi and *Tosephos,* in turn were responses to the needs of

their day. The Talmud was becoming a closed mystery until Rashi explained it so that even we can get a glimpse of it, and the Codes made it possible for minds less majestic than the Talmudic to find and state a final *Halacha* verdict. Neither Rashi nor Rambam "created" in the sense of offering something their predecessors did not have. They offered their contributions to the needs of *their* generation and of later ones. Predecessors did not need commentary or code, any more than *Mishna* sages needed *Gemara* discussion to clarify *Mishna*.

The challenges were not only scholarly ones. There was a collision of cultures time and again—pagan, Greek, Roman, Muslim, medieval European, and in later generations—the challenges of nationalism, the industrial and scientific revolutions, the political upheavals and so on. Rambam's *Guide* was one such response, the classical *Mussar* shortly after was another, *Chassidus* is a more recent one.

There were two challenges at the birth of *Chassidus*, one just past, one looming in the future, threatening though unsuspected. The first were unnerving experiences of the Jewish people, the phony so-called Messiah Shabsai Tzvi and the crushing disillusionment in his wake, and the ravages of the Cossack revolt in the middle 1600's that devastated eastern European Jewry. As the 18th century progressed, the material and spiritual conditions of Jewry in that part of the world were deplorable, ominous.

The other challenge was still ahead, that of the breakdown of the ghetto, the access to western culture suddenly made available to Jews, the more open society that followed the French Revolution and Napoleon's incursions into eastern Europe. These were possibly the most serious challenges our people ever faced, including so many sharp threats to Jewry's simple existence, all converging in full fury simultaneously. *Chassidus*, of course, was not the only response, and that is part of the glory of Torah, its capacity to encompass variety with integrity—but our interest at the moment is *Chassidus*. German Jewry found its Hirsch and

Lithuanian Jewry its Reb Yisrael Salanter and his *Mussar* movement.

Interestingly, the challenge that *Chassidus* addressed itself to in the primitive village world of the Carpathians over two centuries ago is remarkably similar to the challenge of our own generation—estrangement, alienation, Jewish ignorance. The wagonner who could barely read, or couldn't read at all, felt estranged from his heritage, and the sophisticated Jewish artist and scientist at the forefront of culture in New York and London in the 1970's knows dismally little of his heritage and feels its effects on his life minimally if at all.

Chassidus at the outset addressed itself to the incorruptible core, the essence, of the Jew, the self that cannot be alienated. In fact the very statement of this core or essence was a refreshing departure from the conventional thinking. The simple Jew could not be rejected any longer because of his illiteracy and deficiencies in *mitzvah* observance. The relationship between Jew and G-d, symbolic of his relations with Judaism or Torah or his people, assumed a fresh meaning. A child cannot be truly alienated from a parent, except of course externally, superficially. It is an irrevocable relationship in essence. (The difference between the essence and the peripheral is discussed in the essay, "Ahavas Yisrael," as are other elements of this essay, and in "Chassidic Attitudes to Other Jews.")

The Baal Shem Tov based this teaching on Biblical passages and had no need to strain the plain meaning of the text. "You are children of . . . G-d" seems obvious enough, but only when it is translated into attitudes and is used to overcome disdain for another does it assume substance. Let us make this more clear.

"Love your fellow as yourself" is familiar enough to everyone. In the Baal Shem Tov's day, and in practical terms many still seem to share this attitude, this love had to be earned. Some are deserving of this love and others not. The scholarly, the pious, obviously did; the ignorant—and in those days they were legion—were excluded. It was a selective, discriminating love. In effect, the Jewish community was split into two groups, hardly a salutary situation in good conditions, potentially disastrous at that time, and ours.

The alienation the unlettered felt was internal and external, caused both by feelings of inadequacy due to ignorance and poverty, and by rejection by the learned. The Baal Shem Tov's doctrine was not novel but it was revolutionary in terms of his day. "Love your fellow" is not contingent on virtue, nor is it forfeited by deficiencies. The ignorant were embraced by the Baal Shem Tov and his new school, *Chassidus,* and the people responded enthusiastically. They could now claim their share in the legacy of Israel.

Here *Chassidus* responded to challenges, both actual and imminent. The demoralization wrought by Shabsai Tzvi and Chmielnicki's Cossacks on the one hand, and the disintegration of institutions and commitment threatened by Judaism's cultural collision with the West, were both faced by *Chassidus.*

The so-called Emancipation avowedly permitted Jews to enter the general society, but it carried a price-tag, Jews had to rid themselves of their Jewishness. "Everything to the Jew as a man, nothing to the Jew as a Jew," could be a governmental edict or social pressure. The so-called Enlightenment, exposing, even thrusting, Jews to the culture of the West, oppressed many Jews with a feeling of inferiority. "Be a Jew at home, a man in public," hardly makes the Jewish heart swell with pride. It is something to apologize for, rationalize, modify and adapt. Judaism as a religion was now compared to Christianity, and in jaundiced eyes was found wanting. Jewish mores, dress, language, culture, were abandoned in favor of the more "attractive" gentile ways. Even when Judaism was not discarded, it was retained reluctantly, an unavoidable evil.

Chassidus vigorously countered this. The Jew was imbued with a pride in his Jewishness and his personality. A "child of G-d" bearing G-d's own Covenant, is inferior to no one.

Chassidus was strong in Poland, while virtually or actually nonexistent in Germany and France, and assimilation was calamitous there. Comparisons with the peasantry in the East were no threat, but eventually the ideas of the West penetrated eastern Europe and here the fortification of the Jewish spirit was a vital contribution of *Chassidus*.

Chassidus established a hierarchy of values. Torah in general of course did the same, but *Chassidus* translated this into actual living situations. Wealth, social acceptance, recognition by the gentiles, were not the ultimate good. *Neshama*, soul, and its development and flowering were the ideal of life, the measure of a man. All else is ancillary. The soul's fulfillment, life's vindication, was naturally conceived in spiritual terms. Closeness to G-d, effected through devotion to His commandments, transforms a gross Creation into a vehicle for G-dliness. Severance from G-d, rejection of His Torah, corrupts the soul and the world.

An "ordinary" person is not ordinary; no Prince is. His every deed, his words, his thoughts and feelings are critical to his welfare and the well-being of all Creation. Man's importance is cosmic. Creation depends on him. G-d "depends" on him. His integrity is critical, his closeness to G-d, his living by G-d's standards and expectations. Hardships and obstacles do not eclipse G-d; they challenge man to transcend or transform them. The quality of one's life was a paramount concern, while the visible and quantitative were secondary. He may be impoverished and persecuted but even in Exile he is still the Prince.

The Modern period, introduced around the turn of the 18th century and continuing until our day, held out great promise at the start. A Heine could mourn that the passport into the salon is a baptismal certificate, an Uvarov in Russia could concede that his efforts to "enlighten" the benighted Jews of his vast land were designed simply to effect their conversion. Still the allure of the West was not resisted nor were the naive made more skeptical by disillusioning experience. The opposition to *Haskalah* (Enlightenment) in *Chassidic* communities was vigorous, and

15

based, we may infer, on insights drawn from Torah commitment.

I suggest that authentic appreciates authentic, spurious cannot conceive of anything but spurious. The authentic, thoroughly committed Jew was not deluded by the authentic Christian (Uvarovs and Napoleons and the western world in general) and his own commitment, and instinctively if inarticulately stood in implacable opposition to the ultimate dissolution of his people. The "modified" Jew, having left his commitment and fullness in the Jewish world, and not having entered or been accepted into the gentile, could not appreciate what the true promise of the "Modern" world is. He took the declarations for what they said, trustingly, admitting "failings" and backwardness in Judaism as lived in the *shtetl* or city of Galitzia and the Ukraine, meekly assenting to the vicious attacks of the "liberators" of Israel. ("The Tzemach Tzedek and the *Haskalah* Movement" describes a chapter in this history.)

The Baal Shem Tov insisted on penetrating to the interior, the inwardness. He did this in encountering a problem of the Jewish society, and penetrated to the core of the issue—in homely terms, "Is it good for the Jews?" Emancipation and Enlightenment are lofty terms, unassailable, but the *Chassidim* would not be misled by the external charm. They insisted on boring in to the core, and found that the promise was nothing less than the extinction of Israel, the morality and ethics nothing more than an attractively packaged jungle. The modern world is of course not in the past, though so many of its promises have proven to be sterile. *Chassidus* today is still dedicated to dealing with the essence, and perhaps some of its success in addressing the contemporary Jew is a result of this approach.

In both cases, the individual and the communal, *Chassidus* stressed the insoluble bond between Israel and G-d, impervious to the corrosions of swiftly changing circumstances.

*   *   *   *   *   *

WHAT IS CHASSIDUS? WHAT IS CHABAD?

A definition of Chassidus: it is a method of serving G-d, naturally within the Torah framework. At its inception it stressed elements of Torah that were not sufficiently stressed at that time, elements vital to full Jewish living.

At the time of the Baal Shem Tov, the definition of a "good Jew" was the learned Jew, the Talmudist. The primary bridge between man and G-d was the mind. The primary exercise of Judaism was Talmud study. Intellect was *the* religious experience. This had incalculable effects in raising the level of scholarship and the prestige of scholars, particularly in areas like Lithuania where Talmud reigned in unchallenged supremacy. Historians of Torah will doubtless properly rank these communities with the finest in our history. Intellect, we repeat, was the focus.

Apart from the unlearned who were excluded, this also excluded too much of the man himself—specifically, his emotions. The Baal Shem Tov stressed emotion, joy, enthusiasm in G-d's service, and the soaring experience that worship could be. Warm, even passionate worship, with song and gestures (unconscious of course, and certainly unpremeditated or deliberate) became integral to *Chassidus*. The simple Jew could participate in worship without feeling deficient and his sense of closeness to G-d was real and personal. He poured out his heart to G-d, a child addressing a father. To be sure, the Lithuanian Talmudist scrupulously observed the mitzvah of *davening*, but it was clearly secondary in rank to study, and might be regarded as a holy chore to be discharged and then return promptly to one's "real" work—Talmud.

It will be obvious by now that *Chassidus* seemed to address itself to the "masses," especially the ignorant, and to the emotions. What of the mind?

The doctrines of the Baal Shem Tov were sublime and inspiring, but the Alter Rebbe provided an "intellectual" underpinning for them. Lofty statements may be insufficient in themselves, calling for a demonstration of their cohesiveness, their sources. *Chabad* perceives the principles of the Baal Stem Tov not as discrete elements but as a pattern. It provides a perspective that leads ineluctably to these principles. They become rational rather than arbitrary declarations.

Challenges to *Chassidic* statements are easy to formulate—how does one arouse a heart indifferent to worship? Why should a scoundrel be worthy of love? How can I confront a trying, even perilous situation, with equanimity and integrity? And suppose I don't feel "joy"—or any emotion exalted by Torah and *Chassidus*—am I at a dead-end? How control a driving passion or overcome a debilitating character weakness? How reconcile the body's insistent demands for gratification with a soul that refuses to be shackled?

Chassidus, Chabad, regards these as details, not to be handled individually (except perhaps later in one's development) but as part of the wholeness of man. The core, the essence, must be recognized, as apart from the external, the obvious. Then the pattern assumes shape, the solutions and directions accompany the problems.

Kabbalah-Chassidus speak of the attributes of man, and their parallels—the *sephirot,* the Divine attributes. These are generally divided into two groups, the intellectual attributes (*chochmah, binah,* and *daat,* or Wisdom, Understanding and Knowledge), and the seven emotive attributes, the primary ones being *chesed* (kindness and all its extensions) and *gevurah* (severity and all its implications). So-called general *Chassidus,* the developments in Poland and Ukraine, as distinct from *Chabad* which was centered in White Russia and considered "Litvak" by the others, continued to stress the emotions. Without at this point involving ourselves in the issue of integrity with the original Baal Shem Tov doctrine, whether general *Chassidus* is more "authentic" or Chabad which seems to be something of a departure, the Alter Rebbe recognized the limitations of the form *Chassidus* had, and he therefore developed, or shall we say—articulated, a new approach within *Chassidus.*

The Rebbe was not content with compartmentalized service or *Chassidus,* meaning: the devout worshipper serves G-d with his heart; the Talmudist with his mind; even when one person incorporates both *mitzvot,* they have no point of contact. Another "compartment" could be the socially active, energetically practicing hospitality and charity for example. This would be another facet of *Yiddishkeit,* properly observed, but quite distinct from the other facets.

Chabad recognized another need. *Chassidus* appealing to the emotions has a limited appeal. The scholarly would be left cold, indifferent, even hostile, contemptuous. *Chassidus* is not intended for the simple folk any more than Torah is intended for the intellectually gifted. They belong to *all* Israel. To make inroads among the opponents of *Chassidus,* the doctrine must be presented in an intellectually challenging manner. This *Chabad* undertook.

Again a Scriptural quotation served as a foundation for a school. "Know the G-d of your fathers and serve Him with a whole heart" (I Chron. 28:9). There are several immediate inferences: that G-d can be known (to a degree at least); that it is imperative to "know" Him; that this knowledge precedes serving Him with a "whole heart."

How does one go about "knowing" the unknowable? *Chassidus* proposes (again not as an essentially novel approach, but as one integral and active in a system) that a form of knowledge is accessible to the mortal mind. Biblical statements like "From my flesh I perceive G-d" (Job 19:26) and man is created "in the image of G-d" give us points of reference. Studying man gives us insights into G-d; studying G-d gives us a perception of the true nature of humanity. Man knowing himself in this way gains a fresh perspective, a deeper insight into himself and his potential, and becomes a transformed human being.

"Knowing" is an intellectual exercise, not a flash of intuition or a mystical experience. It has its own framework, terminology, pre-suppositions, as does any field of study, and makes the mind central, insists on comprehension, analysis, challenge, articulation, communication. It calls for scholarship, rigorous, demanding. The sheer amount of *Chabad* literature is staggering and its depth can be appreciated only through devoted study.

Then "whole heart" follows, for *moach shalit al halev*, another concept central to *Chabad*, mind has dominion over the heart. Spontaneous emotions, noble and sublime as they may be, are not the works of man, not products of his "service." If one is moved by a surge of love of G-d or man, or is overwhelmed by a sense of insignificance in the presence of G-d's majesty—wonderful. But what if one's heart is recalcitrant, unmoved? "Know the G-d of your fathers," *Chabad* teaches, is the key to "serve Him with a whole heart," regardless of one's tendencies. (The essay "Ahavas Yisroel" develops this theme.)

The point here is that mind and emotion are not truly distinct. They have something of a symbiotic relationship. Mind engenders emotion; emotion validates mind. A mind that truly grasps "How great are Your works" will elicit love or awe in the heart, or else the concept is deficient somehow. In turn, emotion must be translated into the mundanes of living, rather than being a vague abstraction, pleasant enough but ineffectual. Here is a *Chabad* contribution: mind and heart and hand are sequential, associated, integrated. There are no compartments. There is only man, and the different aspects of man, body and soul, mind and heart, actions, personal life and public man, *mitzvah* performance and "ordinary" activities—all are part of man, fortifying each other, harmoniously forming a whole person.

To be sure, the intellectual challenge of *Chabad* is formidable, a challenge to any mind, particularly when the mind challenge is extended to carrying mind into the realms of emotion and prayer, and then into human relationships. *Chassidus* as presented by *Chabad* was now prepared to enrich the Talmudists of Lithuania. While one cannot say that the *Misnagdic* bastions of opposition to *Chassidus* came tumbling down, there were many fresh adherents, and—this must be noted—many of the concepts and practices of *Chassidus* have become "normative" in the Torah community, even among avowed *Misnagdim*.

When the Alter Rebbe was a youth, deciding where to further his Torah education, he had two alternatives— Vilna or Mezritch. Vilna was the Talmud center of the world, Mezritch the seat of *Chassidus.* "In Vilna one learns 'how to learn.' In Mezritch one learns how to *daven,*" was a current aphorism. The Rebbe felt that he had some insights into "learning" but not into *davening,* so he selected Mezritch. We may suggest that his new school of *Chassidus* was similarly designed to answer the needs of other young scholars, to teach them "how to *daven,*" and all the richness of the emotions and soul when harnessed to G-d's service according to the instruction and ideals of *Chassidus.*

Rebbe and Chassid

There is a Torah of ink on parchment, and there is a Torah of flesh and blood. The parchment scroll carries the words of the Torah; so, too, the Rebbe, a man of flesh and blood, acts as a bearer of the words of the Torah. Perhaps, for the *Chassid,* the Rebbe represents an image of what the human product of Torah should be. If a person could fulfill all the ideals of the Torah, what sort of human being would he become? Picture a person who is completely devoted to Torah, who lives the teachings of Torah, whose thoughts are Torah thoughts, and whose ideals are Torah ideals, an utterly selfless man, whose every word and act is an expression not of self but of Torah. This, the *Chassid* says, is the Rebbe.

But this seems a little unrealistic. How can we expect so much of a mortal? Let us turn to the *Mishna,* which urges us to "Nullify your will before His will." This is not simply a matter of subordinating your will to G-d's will; according to this precept, your will does not even *exist* in the presence of G-d's will. What you want should be only what G-d wants. A man who lives up to this ideal has no desires of his own. Too idealistic, you say? The *Mishna* is not given to flowery rhetoric. When it insists that man should "nullify" his own will before the will of G-d, it is expressing a demand that is not impossible for a human being to fulfill. Without straining modesty, we can declare that we have not even begun to approach that ideal. It is ridiculous even to speak of it. But does this mean that it is impossible to attain? Obviously, it *is* possible, since Torah demands it. How many people succeed in reaching it? We do not know, but we know that it can be done. Every generation produces a *tzaddik* who has attained the ideal set forth in the *Mishna*.

This, the *Chassid* says, is the Rebbe.

As he observes the Rebbe, hears him speak, studies his words, the *Chassid* is constantly reinforced in his conviction that his Rebbe has succeeded in attaining the level of "nullifying his own will." Is this conviction "faith in the Rebbe"? *Emunat tzaddikim,* faith in the *tzaddik,* is a doctrine expressed in the Torah itself and hence one of the norms of Judaism. But *emunat tzaddikim* is a faith grounded in reason and experience, not an exercise in credulity.

People often ask, "How can a *Chassid* have so much faith in the Rebbe?" For my part, I would wonder not so much about how a *Chassid* can accept the Rebbe so completely but more about the other side of the coin, how the Rebbe can be so utterly devoted to his *Chassidim*. This is what I can't understand, that the *Chassid's* devotion to the Rebbe is only a pale reflection of what the Rebbe feels for each of his *Chassidim.*

Take a simple everyday example. The Rebbe has thousands upon thousands of Chassidim. It is no exaggeration to say that he knows the name of every one of them; that he knows about their children, their families, their strengths and weaknesses, their personalities and their problems. And he is concerned about the welfare of every single *Chassid* no less than parents are concerned about their children. Any *Chassid* who comes to see the Rebbe for *yechidus,* to spend a little time alone with him, or who receives a letter from the Rebbe in answer to an inquiry or a request for advice, can see that the Rebbe is as close to a *Chassid* as one human being can be to another. Now multiply that by thousands upon thousands . . .

The variety of problems which the *Chassid* brings to the Rebbe is as wide as the spectrum of problems the *Chassid* faces in his lifetime: problems of business, health, marriage, child-rearing, education, where to live—and in all these questions the *Chassid* will take counsel with the Rebbe before making his decision. People who are not *Chassidim* themselves find this difficult to understand. Why discuss such questions with the Rebbe? It is generally accepted that people consult a rabbi, or a rebbe, when they are faced with "religious" problems—questions of faith, prayer, self-discipline or interpretations of the Law. But why go to a rebbe with such "worldly" concerns as a job, an operation, or a new home?

It is not as strange as it would seem to the non-*Chassid* at first glance. Torah Judaism stresses that every phase of life must bear the stamp of religion, that nothing in the Jewish experience can be alien to the religious experience, that the Torah has something to say about every facet of human life. There are many problems that do not seem to have religious connotations, but the manner in which they are dealt with will have a powerful impact on the religious lives of those concerned.

A young man of, say, 16 or 18 has several choices of career open before him. Should he continue going to the yeshiva—perhaps enter the rabbinate or the field of Jewish education—or should he begin training for business, or one of the professions? The question seems "neutral" enough, but the young man's decision will have a crucial effect on his future religious life. Whom should he marry? On the face of it, this is a highly personal question, apparently unrelated to "religion"; yet there are few decisions that will have a more profound influence on the rest of the lives of the two young people involved.

When the *Chassid* takes these problems to the Rebbe, he does so with good reason. He is certain that the Rebbe knows all the aspects of the problem and knows what the Torah has to say. The *Chassid* is certain, too, that the Rebbe is selfless enough to tell him not what he, the Rebbe, might personally prefer, but only what the Torah would have the Rebbe say. The guidance which the *Chassid* receives from the Rebbe is an expression of what the Torah would want this person to do under these particular circumstances.

There is yet another facet of the Rebbe's devotion to his *Chassidim.* We have already mentioned *yechidus,* the private meeting which the *Chassid* has with the Rebbe to discuss what is closest to his own heart. Rebbes throughout the generations have noted that probably the most physically exhausting aspect of *yechidus* is the necessity for the Rebbe to place himself into the situation of the *Chassid* and then, as soon as this *Chassid* has left, to place himself into the position of the next *Chassid* who has *yechidus* with the Rebbe, and so on. The Rebbe must constantly find an area of common ground with the *Chassid* before him, to search his own life's experience for something which, albeit in a subtle and refined form, might address itself to the situation or problem faced by the *Chassid* who has come to seek his advice. What the *Chassid* has gone through is not alien to the Rebbe. The Rebbe has perfect empathy with the *Chassid*; he is in the "same" situation. The Rebbe can truly feel the *Chassid's* anguish, his distress and indecision.

Quite apart from anything the Rebbe may say to the *Chassid,* the feeling that comes across so strongly and profoundly is, "Here is a person completely devoted to me, one who cares deeply about what troubles me." It is only natural, then, that a *Chassid* with any degree of sensitivity will respond to the devotion that the Rebbe has shown him.

*   *   *   *   *   *

The term "Rebbe" describes not only a person but a relationship. that between the Rebbe and the *Chassid*. It might not be presumptuous to suggest that the Rebbe is Rebbe to the degree that the *Chassid* is *Chassid*. It is clear, of course, that we are not discussing the Rebbe objectively, or in terms of himself as an individual, but solely in terms of what the Rebbe means to the *Chassid*—the existential Rebbe, the subjective Rebbe, as it were.

The classic *Chassid*-Rebbe relationship is primarily spiritual. Not that any aspect of the *Chassid's* life is ever divorced from his *Chassidus,* but the center of his existence is his soul, and not, as might be the case with others, an external factor such as his career. The *Chassid* is devoted to the study of *Chassidus*, and the Rebbe is his teacher. The

Chassid endeavors to *daven* according to the *Chassidic* ideal, and the Rebbe is his mentor. The *Chassid* is concerned with his inner development—his "I", his relations with G-d and man, his shortcomings, his potential, and the Rebbe is his guide.

Note: This does not mean that the *Chassid* expects the Rebbe to study Torah for him, or to *daven* for him, or to be a "saint" in his stead. The Rebbe does not act as the representative, or intermediary, or the surrogate of the *Chassid*. The *Chassid* must sow the seeds himself, as it were, by the toil of his own heart and mind. The Rebbe then provides the *b'racha*, the blessing, the "rain" that causes the seeds to sprout and to bear rich fruit.

Naturally, the "total *Chassid*", while by no means thank G-d a rarity, is not an everyday phenomenon. But *Chassidus* is not elitist, or exclusive. Others, less dedicated, may properly be regarded as *Chassidim* and enjoy as deep and close a relationship with the Rebbe as they themselves determine. It may only be an occasional relationship—a visit in times of trouble, or a request for advice or a blessing. The decision is the *Chassid's*.

* * * * * *

The early *Chassidim*—the followers of the first *Chabad* Rebbe*—compared their regard for the Rebbe with the regard the Children of Israel had held for Moses. Maimonides notes that it was not miracles such as the Ten Plagues or the crossing of the Red Sea that inspired Israel to believe in Moses. The promise "they will believe in you eternally" (Ex. 19:9) could be fulfilled only after they "serve G-d on this mountain" (Ex. 3:12). Israel came to believe in Moses because he taught them the Torah, how to serve G-d. In the same manner, the Rebbe was Rebbe because he taught his disciples Torah, how to serve G-d. This, we may presume, is the role in which the Rebbe sees himself in preference to any other: to teach the *Chassidic* community, and the individual *Chassid*, how to serve G-d.

* * * * * *

*R. Shneur Zalman of Liadi (1745-1813), known as the Alter Rebbe, the "Old" Rebbe.

We have already noted that the *Chassid* considers the question of his career as one which should be brought before the Rebbe. The *Chassid* believes that the life of every man has a unique purpose, though that purpose may be concealed from him. In order to fulfill our true calling, we must make the right choices from among many alternatives. The Prophet Jonah was faced with two choices— either to proceed to Nineveh to exhort the sinful people there, or to retreat to Tarshish. Nineveh meant fulfillment of his Divine calling; Tarshish, an escape from the purpose of his existence. For Jonah, the course he had to follow was clear.

Most of us are likely to base our decisions on self-interest and limited vision. But the decisions we make are crucial. The rabbinate and medicine are both noble callings, but the young man we mentioned will exert one sort of influence on his environment if he chooses to become a doctor, but quite another if he decides to become a rabbi. No matter what his eventual choice, the *Chassid* knows that his existence has a purpose, and that he has a mission to fulfill. His unspoken question is, "What does G-d expect of me?" We cannot easily find the answer. We are too close to ourselves, and perhaps too far removed from G-d. That is why a *Chassid* has a Rebbe.

The *Chassid* knows that his Rebbe's vision is neither limited as is his own, nor influenced by self-interest. *Chassidic* men and women will cheerfully travel across the globe—to Australia, South Africa, and also to less exotic places—simply because that is their Nineveh; these are the places where they will justify their lives.

* * * * * *

But what, after all, is a Rebbe? Is he a scholar? Yes, he is; but he is more than that. Is he a *tzaddik*? He is that, too, but he is more. If this gives you the impression that I really cannot answer the question, please do not imagine that this is not deliberate on my part. Let me explain. A mind can grasp only that which is within its reach. Man can comprehend that which is smaller than himself. But he will

27

never be able to understand that which exceeds his own limited stature. A Sage once said, "If I were able to know G-d, then I would be G-d." The answer to the rhetorical question, "Who can appreciate the greatest mathematician in the world?" is, "Only another mathematician of equal stature." Who can appreciate, or even describe, a Rebbe? Only another Rebbe, his peer. But although we cannot describe what a Rebbe *is*, we are able to say what he means to *us,* and this I will attempt to do by referring to a letter the Rebbe once wrote.

The Rebbe described a *halacha* in *Chabad* terms, specifically, the laws of *mikvah* and *ma'ayan*. The *mikvah* is a pool of water in which an impure body or object can be immersed and purified. A *ma'ayan* is a wellspring which serves the same function. However, the laws governing the two are not identical. The *mikvah* must contain a minimum amount of water (the Talmud uses the measure of 40 *s'ah*, roughly 200 gallons). If the *mikvah* contains less water than these minimum 40 measures, it is not only incapable of fulfilling its purifying function but is in danger of becoming defiled itself by contact with an impure object. The *ma'ayan,* by contrast, need not hold a minimum quantity of water; any amount is sufficient to purify.

The *mikvah* must have walls that retain water so that no water is perceptibly lost. If the *mikvah* wall happens to have a crack, allowing water to seep out, then the *mikvah* is not kosher, no matter how much water it contains. The *ma'ayan,* on the other hand, is subject to no such restriction; it can lose water all the time without thereby losing its purifying function.

The explanation of these difference is: a *mikvah* is a self-contained entity; a *ma'ayan,* on the other hand, is connected to its source.

This analogy may also be applied to two distinct types of Jews. The *mikvah* type may be quite capable of purifying others and remaining pure himself, but in order to do so, he must satisfy certain stringent requirements. He must possess a clear minimum of learning and piety and, even more difficult, must be exceedingly careful to preserve whatever scholarship or religious zeal he has. When he leaves the shelter of the Yeshiva and becomes involved in worldly affairs, he must be constantly on guard against the inevitable loss of undeflected devotion to Torah that comes with entry into everyday life.

Not so the *ma'ayan* type. This Jew need not have the minimum of spiritual qualities that the *mikvah* type must possess, and he may lose from even that small amount. But this does not affect his ability to purify others and to remain pure himself, because he has preserved his attachment to a never-ceasing sourch of living waters. This is the *Chassid* who has a Rebbe. The wisdom of this *Chassid* is not limited to his own intellect; his piety is not circumscribed by his petty considerations; his achievements and his impact on his environment are not derived solely from his own efforts; his ability to maintain his Jewish and *Chassidic* integrity, to resist the attrition of his surroundings, is not due to his own fortitude. He credits everything he has accomplished to the fact he has remained attached to a source. Pragmatically, the most effective *Chassidim*, the Rebbe's "shock troops," quite apart from their knowledge of *Chassidus* and Talmud, are distinguished for their devotion to the Rebbe.

Here, then, is one definition of a Rebbe. He is a source that never fails. The *Chassid* who maintains a bond with his Rebbe is never alone; though continents and oceans may separate him from his Rebbe, he never feels that he has been cut adrift. As the late Rebbe once put it, "Oceans do not separate us; they connect us."

Aloneness can take many forms. When rabbis meet, particularly in remote isolated Jewish communities, "aloneness" seems to be the constant refrain. Here, the need is for something more than mere encouragement, or even the wise counsel of an elder. The *Chassid* listens, sympathizes and murmurs a grateful blessing to his Creator that he, the *Chassid*, has a source of living waters, and that he and his source are so close to one another . . .

Speak English . . .
But Think Jewish

(from a discussion with students in a Jewish fraternity)

Shabbos is a "sign" and *tefillin* are called a "sign" (and, incidentally, since a second sign is redundant, we don't wear *tefillin* on Shabbos). A "sign" indicates uniqueness, distinctiveness. A significant aspect of Shabbos and *tefillin* would be their symbolism of the distinctive bond that joins Israel and G-d. As the sign is neglected the uniqueness becomes blurred.

We live in a world that constantly impinges on us, whose atmosphere is so permeated with its particular values and attitudes and presumptions, that we absorb them without effort, unknowingly, unaware that we are being influenced. The American Jew is numerically a tiny 2% or 3% of America. Identifiably Jewish values, distinct and different from those of the other 98%, are so submerged, so unfamiliar to the "average" American Jew, that he doesn't know any exist and certainly cannot share in them. Culturally, the Jew is thoroughly—shall we say—Western, for that is a neutral sounding term. Actually, the culture, the values, the premises of Western culture are not "neutral." They are to a tremendous degree Christian, and even if only in origin, nonetheless those roots are hardly obscure.

In the unquestioned, subterranean presuppositions of religion, in those basic statements that precede any discussion of religion, Christianity's views are a part of the West, for in religion the West is Christian. There is nothing improper about this, nothing to criticize, but the Jew should realize the origin, the orientation of his views. He ought to know that they are not universal, that they are specifically doctrinal, and that they are not in consonance with his own doctrines. In other words, I suggest that the American Jew conceives of religion and discusses it in Christian terms. He grapples with religious difficulties, because a Jew must examine Judaism, but he does so with Christian categories. His conflict is not necessarily a Jewish one, but one of reconciling divergent viewpoints, the Jewish and the Christian, that were never intended to be reconciled, for they represent thoroughly different values. The "sign" of the Jew has been neglected, the demarcation between Jewish and non-Jewish faiths has been blurred, and the unaware Jew rejects or scorns his own religion because he does not have the tools for handling it appropriately.

Reb Shmuel, the teacher of Chassidus when I learned in Lubavitch, used to say that sometimes we have a question and an answer, but the question is still a question. Sometimes, after the answer we have no question. He illustrated, "I might ask a boy, 'Why were you late for class?' Even when he answers that he overslept, the question is still a question. But when the boy answers, 'I was not late. I came on time,' then there is no question left." I propose that many of the challenges of Judaism, many of the questions about Torah and mitzvos can be answered, not by answering the question, not by accepting its initial assumptions, but by eliminating the questions, by giving a fresh perspective, a view that makes the question irrelevant.

Conventional thinking illustrates these adoptions from Christian thought, and they are often adopted, not adapted. The Rabbi is regarded as the Jewish equivalent of the minister or priest, the synagogue parallels the church, Shabbos is the Jewish version of Sunday, the Jew and Christian define faith in the same way though the content of the faith differs,* and so on.

Kashrut is challenged constantly, and I find it interesting that the sophisticated professor and the illiterate laborer

---

*See "Emunah: The Role of Faith in Judaism." Another example of inappropriate adoption of concepts is discussed in "An Accident of Birth."

challenge it in virtually the same words. "In the olden days kosher laws protected the people from trichinosis and such terrible things, but nowadays we have government inspection, and hygiene, and refrigeration, and so *kashrut* is obsolete." The defender of *kashrut* will struggle with all sorts of refutations, with intricate rationales, all trying to convince the questioner that *kashrut* is indeed necessary and relevant and is not obsolete—and the challenger walks off unmoved. He framed his question in particular terms and it was answered in those terms. But those terms are only the verbalization, the tip of the iceberg. He is bothered by something far deeper. Treating the symptoms of his religious malaise will not help him.

Man is a composite, if you will permit a commonplace for a moment, of body and soul, of a wide range of faculties and talents. His body is "lower" than his "spirit," the intellectual is superior to the manual—I don't propose these as my statements, but as those of our culture, those of the pervasive Christianity. The body is scorned as an instrument of G-dliness, as an avenue to heights of spirit. It is ballast, deadweight, the anvil around the neck, the burden. The blessed, the truly dedicated, will spurn the flesh. The celibate is an ideal, the monastery is the religious institution. I know that the liberal will not subscribe to these statements baldly, but they are normative in Christianity. Even in rejecting Puritanism, the libertine is simply a reverse of the Puritan coin, still chafing under that onerous yoke, despite his desperate efforts at hedonism.

However much our liberal will protest this caricature, it is reflected in his religious life. "Good Christian" refers to one who attends church regularly, every Sunday. He must have faith, however their internal groupings define that faith. Works may or may not be critical—let them fight it out. But we'll get back to faith later.

Note what happens when we observe the "good Christian," the representative of religion in the Western world. He has consecrated a place for this worship. He has a day consecrated to serving G-d. Of the countless abilities man has he has dedicated some for Divine service—prayer, faith, understanding, song—the "higher" faculties of man. And then, he has selected one person to stand apart and above, in a sacerdotal position, who is (theoretically) totally dedicated to the Divine service—his clergyman. What a snug, symmetrical compartment for religion. In Time—a day; in Space—a building; in Man—his mind and heart; in Mankind—a cleric.

What now, is the appropriate, meaningful way to pray, to serve G-d, to be "religious"? Through prayer, through faith, through worship and song. From your throat up you are G-d's; G-d alone knows who owns the rest. "What goes out of your mouth is important, not what goes in"—who made that statement? It was an initial step in breaking away from Judaism and founding a new faith. We should know that. Here is the real question about *kashrut*, the assumptions that lead to the challenge.

One can understand Judaism insisting on prayers, on *Sh'ma*, on faith and on charity, our questioner is really saying, but what is this business about food? You can serve G-d with your mind and your emotions, with your "higher" faculties, but not with a base animal function, not with your suppers. Since dietary laws "cannot" be religious, then they *must* have some other origin and significance, logically hygiene. If that justification was warranted thirty centuries ago, it is anachronistic today. This is the challenge to *kashrut*. Until the American Jew stops thinking in these Christian categories of what is legitimate and authentic religious experience and service, he will never be able to meaningfully accept mitzvot, or Judaism for that matter. He must learn to think like a Jew and stop thinking like a Christian. The next man's ideas may be perfectly valid for *him*, but they are not mine.

Well, what *does* Judaism have to say about serving G-d and authentic religious experience? There may be a single word to sum up Judaism, and of course that word must be understood—totality. All the man, all the time, in every place, under all circumstances, in every activity, in every fiber of his being—can serve G-d, can apprehend Him, can communicate with Him. "Nothing human is alien to me," said a sage; nothing human is alien to Torah, to G-d, to Judaism. Whatever the Jew does can be a channel, a bridge, between himself and G-d, or it can be a barrier, a wall separating him from G-d, an act to smother his sensitivity, to coarsen him.

Certainly mind is part of man. Spirit, song, faith—these are all human, so these are all legitimate experiences of G-d's closeness. But so is man's food, and his business and recreation, and his family, and his disappointments and ambitions, and fears and envies and gladness, and his esthetics. The mind and heart are avenues to G-d, true, so are food and family life. This is the meaning of totality— nothing is excluded from the purview of Torah. There is nothing intrinsically "higher" and "lower."

On Yom Kippur eve, in a shul jammed with worshippers, covering your eyes and crying out *Sh'ma Yisroel,* meaning and feeling every word in the depths of the heart—this is worship, this is religious feeling. Anyone will subscribe to that. Torah tells us that at the breakfast table, on an ordinary Tuesday, we can serve G-d just as well, when we eat as He tells us, when our meal is more than a satisfaction of appetite, when we are conscious of a *bracha* before and *bentching* after, with a *yarmulka,* with *kashrut*—this is an altar, sacred, man addressing G-d in a language other than words alone—and G-d sees and hears. Does that sound a bit far-fetched? Here's a more easily digestible illustration. A piece of animal hide can be used for various purposes. One can cut out a piece of shoe leather and use the adjacent piece for a Torah parchment. The Torah parchment is leather, brute physical matter—but it becomes holy. We revere it, embrace it, stand in its presence. What has happened to this piece of animal skin? We used it for a "higher" purpose, endowed it with a quality not inherent within it, and it transcends its materiality. Everything we encounter can become a "Torah scroll" when we use it properly, as Torah prescribes.

This is thinking like a Jew, shedding the categories and presumptions of the overwhelming Christian environment. The distinctiveness may be difficult to maintain, the integrity of Jewish ideas may become diluted under constant battering by the environment, so we have "signs" to remind us of what we are. Let others decide for themselves what is religion for them, what will ennoble them, make them aware of G-d. We have no quarrel with that. All we insist is that we have our own standards, our ideals, our conceptions, our communication with G-d, our awareness of His concern for us. Because Christianity scorns the flesh is no reason for us to be upset about *kashrut.* We pray in many languages, in the language of the mind and the heart and the hand and the family and whatever we do. Which is the "superior" service of G-d? Who cares? We're not keeping score. We are living. On Yom Kippur we serve G-d one way. At the office we serve Him in another. With our family life we serve him and in our intellectual pursuits we serve Him—the total Jew serves Him.

Now, what was that question about *kashrut?* Isn't it obsolete now with government inspection? What in the world does government inspection have to do with the total human experience being a religious opportunity? We need not answer the question of the obsoleteness of *kashrut.* All we need is to examine our preconceptions, and re-affirm our Jewish perspective. The question disappears.

Three Stages

(Remarks delivered to a convention of the Lubavitcher Women's Organization, Neshei Chabad.)

Faulty Communication or Faulty Values?

The term "Generation Gap" has become a familiar part of the language, deploring the "lack of communication" between the young and their elders, between parents and children, teachers and students. It is a cliche, but it would never have become so common without a sizable amount of justification.

Every generation sows its wild oats; youth has its traditional fling; distress about what "the younger generation is coming to" seems to be expected and ritualistic; the mature look to the future with anxiety when they consider the flightly youth to whom tomorrow has been entrusted. Probe a bit, we are told by the more optimistic types, question the old-timers about their own younger days, and they will admit and even boast about their youthful exploits. But we should not be overly complacent about the conflict between the generations that exists today. It goes beyond the inevitable conventional disagreements. It is not necessarily a harmless "phase." Something irreversible may be happening, something valuable destroyed beyond repair. There is a disquieting truth about the chasm between fathers and sons.

History is the account of how values have been transmitted from generation to generation, how wisdom gleaned from tragedy and success has passed on and how the past has been utilized in coping with the present. Perpetuation of values is the dream of the parent, and effective communication is the key to its fulfillment. We cannot expect perfect value transplantation, because values become obsolete and new values are born all the time. Under some circumstances, a son who followed in his father's footsteps as a farmer or a miner made his parents proud; under other conditions parents rejoice when their children go on to bigger and better things. Still, there are certain values which we cherish as enduring and whose erosion we consider disturbing and even tragic. "New moralities" became a fad: we pray that they pass as swiftly as they came upon the scene, but they will leave countless scarred lives in their wake. With all its faults, democracy is no worse than any other system of government we have seen; therefore, we cannot regard attacks on democracy with equanimity and the placid confidence that "this, too, shall pass." Morality and democracy, once lost, are not easily regained.

The Jew concerned with the quality of Jewish life is uneasy about more than illiteracy and empty synagogues, grave though these symptoms are. We have become accustomed to expecting less from the child than from the parent. But the issue today is far deeper than "a little more" or "a little less."

"Where have I failed?" is the despairing cry of the father. "It's lack of communication between the generations," someone mumbles. The immigrant generation did indeed have a problem of communication. It was a simple problem of language; parents and children did not have a common background. But today's parents and children do have reasonably common cultural, educational and social backgrounds. Under these circumstances, inability to communicate would present a virtually insoluble problem. But I suggest that, today, there is no problem of communication at all between parents and children. If anything, the parents communicate all too clearly.

Our problem is not one of faulty *communication,* but one of faulty *values.* To understand the problem better, I suggest that there are three stages in the process of value transmittal, stages which we can observe both in the development of American society in general and of American Jewish society in particular.

The values one generation hands down to the next encompass two distinct elements: substance and validation. The parent teaches the substance of a given order of values—say, a concept of right and wrong. Along with these values, he communicates to his children the ideological underpinnings of this concept, the authority that originally proclaimed and hence validates this particular code or system of values. When the child challenges the values taught him by his parents, "Who said so? Why should I accept this?" the parents have a ready answer, which the child accepts. This is Stage One, where code and validation coalesce.

In Stage Two, the child may question, or even reject, the authority but for some reason he preserves the code of values they have taught him, and transmits it to the next generation. When he in turn is challenged to justify the code he seeks a new explanation to justify continued adherence.

In Stage Three, the younger generation rejects not only the authority underlying the code but the values themselves, and the entire code of which these values are a part.

Let us examine America society in general, and then American Jewish society in particular, in this frame of reference.

Early American society was based largely on the Biblical ethos. Religious ideals were recognized and revered at least formally; the Puritan or Protestant outlook colored American life and values. A separation of Church and State might have been declared officially but religion and everyday life were not two separate things in early America. True, there were plenty of scoundrels, but there was a distinction between the honest man and the thief. The Eighth Commandment, "Thou shalt not steal," was a precept of human decenty which was passed from one generation to the next.

If the younger generation demanded, "Who says it's wrong to steal?" the reply of the elders was swift and unequivocal, "G-d, of course." (Obviously, this is gross oversimplification, but the example of values and their supporting authority is clear.) Marital fidelity, respect for one's elders, regard for the rule of law and the ideal of justice—all these were based firmly on an undisputed authority. This was Stage One in the moral history of American civilization.

But as time passed, the authority came under attack from many quarters. The popularization of Darwinism, the acceptance of Biblical criticism with unscientific zeal, the development of cultural anthropology and the study of differing cultures and values—all these tended to challenge the authority. G-d and the Bible became "irrelevant" in the determination of right and wrong. The agnostic cavalierly dismissed faith in G-d, but he still presented a perfectly admirable statement of social conscience. By and large, the moral code was still identical with that based on the values of religion. But the authority cited in its support was no longer G-d, but man. Man and society determined right and wrong. Polygamy might be wrong in one society, but right in another. Morality was a relative concept. This was Stage Two.

The spokesmen of Stage Two—the *fin de siecle* generation—had been reared in Stage One, had imbibed its attitudes, and drawn from its reservoir of values and teachings. The Stage Two generation had been the product of an ethical society based on religious faith. They continued to cherish the values they had been taught—honesty, human decency, concern for one's fellow man. Their barbs were directed only at the foundation for these values. They insisted that the Eighth Commandment (and the code of which this was a part) had not been proclaimed by G-d but formulated by men as they strove to fulfill their finer human potential. Consensus and culture, not an absolute authority, decreed right and wrong. Man and circumstances change, and moral concepts change along with them. There was no longer such a thing as "absolute right" or "absolute wrong."

The Stage Two generation did not fear moral anarchy, for they were confident that there was a basic, rock-bottom morality which would endure. Trifles, petty mores, social conventions might change, but those values that were truly timeless would endure. Man's high—and supposedly still-developing—sense of ethics and morality was considered an adequate, dependable guide. Man did not need to look beyond his own intellectual and moral resources for instruction and justification. There was no danger that moral relativism would degenerate into blatant amorality, for, after all, man had some righteous stirrings of conscience, some instinctive sense of good and evil. Men could be "good" without being "religious," organized religion became expendable, a relic. "Can't a man be good without going to church?" clergymen were asked over and over again. It must be said that the response of the clergy was something less than overwhelmingly persuasive.

Stage Two was marked by an indomitable optimism, based not on faith in G-d, but on a sturdy confidence in man. Despite frequent evidence of backsliding, that generation saw a general upward trend in the course of man's moral history. It was convinced that man progressed not only in science and technology but also in morals and ethics. The carnage in the trenches of 1914-18 gave it some pause, but the faith in man persisted.

While, of course, the boundaries cannot be neatly articulated, we might say that Stage Three had its beginnings following the Second World War. That was the generation which rejected not only the authority for the values in which it had been reared, but the values as such.

Let us stress again that while the generation of Stage Two challenged the authority on which values were based, it did accept the values. It denied the authority of the Bible, but accepted Biblical morality. It might have denied the existence of a personal G-d, but it adhered to ethics. It rejected worship, but retained goodness.

But in Stage Three, the target shifted. That generation not only rejected the authority but also questioned the values. An Englishman who worked with young people succinctly summed up the change that had taken place between 1935 and 1955. "They used to ask, 'Can't you be good without the Church?' Now they ask, 'Why be good?' " Doctrines, codes and values do not stand independently. They stem from definite origins. When the original authority on which they were based is rejected, they demand some new validation, or else eventually the doctrines themselves will be discarded.

Nowadays, when the young ask, "Why be honest, or moral?" the elders may reply, "Because society says we must." The mentor is confident in the collective good sense of "society." But the young start shooting from all directions. How about Nazi Germany? Wasn't that a "society" too? Another, the rugged individualist, refues to accept the dictates of his peers. Why then should he pay attention to arbitrary rules set down by "society"? Besides, who, exactly, is taking the "morality census"? Certainly, a "society" institutes regulations so that its members may live together in ordinary safety, but these are merely "regulations." The term "moral" implies something far more profound and imperative than prudence.

The humanist and the agnostic were heirs to a tradition which they did not create. The human dignity that was considered inalienable yesterday is hardly regarded as sacrosanct today. Decency is not inescapably inherent within man. Modern "civilized" societies have sanctioned and encouraged murder, slavery, immorality, robbery, and every inhuman viciousness. Will anyone guarantee that it cannot happen again tomorrow? In 1930 any sane man would have laughed at predictions of concentration camps, if indeed anyone could have had such a wild imagination. My, how we have progressed in one single generation!

Consensus, society, community-created morality—these could and did result in the perfectly logical conclusion that the State is the ultimate good, with human beings as the pawns and instruments of that State, with no prerogatives or rights, even to life itself, superior to those of the State.

What values are immune to attack today? The family? Marital fidelity? Or perhaps respect for the person or property of another? Life itself? Or the self-respect of being a contributing member of society rather than merely a consuming parasite? What was revered yesterday is fair prey for the iconoclast today, regardless of the consequences. And all this is done with approval of "society."

Our belligerent young continue the challenge. Morality and ethics are human, and hence fallible. If I happen to disapprove, why should I bother with them at all, especially if conformity involves some inconvenience or forces me to forego some breath-taking delight? What is immoral about ignoring conventions and scorning public approval—and indeed, is there more than that to morality in Stage Three?

Yet our world is not entirely depraved. Hitler was fought and destroyed. Injustice is protested and, however haltingly, corrected. The Nazi is not the paragon whom modern man strives to emulate. But this is so only because we still draw from a reservoir of culture and values that has not yet been depleted. We still retain redeeming elements from Stage Two, and even, to a degree, from Stage One. However, we must understand that this reserve is not inexhaustible or eternal. The child who is cut off from it has no moral moorings left, and when he realizes this he may cry out in bitter protest.

We might understand something of yesterday's Flower Children or hippies in this way. They carried the ideas of their teachers to their logical conclusion. They rejected "society" just as their parents once rejected a higher Authority. They scorned possessions and creature comforts and indeed, why should such material things be considered ideals? They are literally adrift morally, recognizing no such thing as right or wrong. Whatever you want is "right." Whatever you don't want is "wrong." They sneer at the hypocrisy of the world of their elders and want no part of it. They may be imprudent, "bad" members of society, but by what standard can they be called immoral?

It is so easy to denounce the parents. They timidly hid behind the skirts of "broadmindedness" and "modernity." When they were asked for guidance, or confronted with decisions, they found an easy refuge in telling their offspring, "Do whatever you feel is right, son. I just want you to be happy." But at the risk of an irrelevant digression, might the responsibility not be shared by the intellectuals who preached without regard for the consequences of their ideas, by the media of entertainment which apparently adopted the code that anything is acceptable as long as it is salable, perhaps even by clergymen who reflected every latest intellectual and social fad instead of demonstrating the fallacies surrounding them?

The question today is not one of this or that "morality." The issue is whether there is any morality at all. If there is a concept of morality, we are forced to defend it or it will fall. If we are prepared for that, if we refuse to recognize that morality must have a foundation, then we must translate such phenomena as Storm Troops and hippies into terms of our own young people. For, unpleasant as it may be, that is the meaning of Stage Three in which our own world finds itself today.

The Jewish World

Let us turn now to the American Jew. Here too we may arbitrarily mark off three stages: (1) the Eastern European, from which most of us hark; (2) the immigrant generation of our parents and grandparents; and (3) the indigenous American Jew, the "young people" of our own day.

The Jewish life of the fabled *shtetl* was thoroughly religious in form and inspiration. People lived by religious faith and commitment. *Tefillin* and charity, Shabbos and hospitality were equally representative of their religion. Why keep *kashrus*? Because the Torah tells us so. Who gave the Torah? G-d, of course. The values and their validation

43

were fused. Sobriety, learning, human concern, these were as much part of the religious values of the *shtetl* as the meticulous observance of ritual. The problem of Jewish identity could not possibly occur to anyone. This picture is, of course, somewhat idealized, but not excessively so.

Stage Two could be that watershed of the American Jewish community, the decades of massive immigration that straddled the turn of the 20th Century. The immigrants were not distinguished by any passionate devotion to Torah and religion. The Yiddish language flourished, the labor movement and social progress became lastingly associated with the Jews of those days. Fathers who could barely sign their names had sons with Ph.D's. Jewish values persisted in strength, but for a new reason. Religion was not the motive force; something new was proposed: "secular" Jewishness. Remember that old Yiddish song: *"Vos mir zeinen zeinen mir, ober yidn zeinen mir"* (We are whatever we are, but we're Jews)? Jewish identity was strong, but the definition of religion had been abandoned. Love of learning, concern for humanity—those classic "Jewish" virtues, had been preserved, but the authority on which they had been based had become hazy with the loss of historic justification. The values survived, but without their validation.

The immigrant had a good memory; his nostalgia was unimpaired. In the Old World he had drawn liberally from a vast reservoir of attitudes and feelings which he cherished. But the tragedy was that now, in the New World, he was cut off from that reservoir. *Licht bentchen* (lighting the Sabbath candles), Elul (the solemn month preceding the Holy Day Season), Simchas Torah (the joyous climax to the Holy Day Season), a good *maggid* (itinerant preacher)—these were remembered with warmth and appreciation, but quite apart from their religious significance. The immigrant felt perfectly "Jewish" without religious observance; he was, as he so frequently put it, a good Jew "at heart." He insisted that he could be, and that he was, a "good Jew" even without *tallis* and *tefillin*. But perhaps the immigrant did not realize why he had been able to remain a Jew at all. Knowingly or not, he was sustained by the religious heritage of the generation before him.

The result was Stage Three—the children and grandchildren of that immigrant generation. We are dealing with them today. The Stage Three youth is not bothered about *tefillin*—chances are he does not even know what *tefillin* are. If anything, he wonders why he should bother "being Jewish" at all. His question is not, "Can't I be a good *Jew* without *religion*?" It is, "Can't I be a good *person* without being Jewish?" The nostalgia and the memories from which his immigrant grandparents had taken their spiritual sustenance are about as close to him as Tibet, and about as relevant. He is as cavalier about dismissing the values of Judaism themselves as his father was about rejecting their religious validation. "Who says so?" is his challenge, and with this he cheerfully jettisons every aspect of his Judaism—including his Jewish identity.

Our progression, if that is the proper word, through Stages One, Two, and Three is clear enough. A system, moral or cultural, must have the support of its source, the foundations upon which it rests. Cut off from its roots, even the most beautiful blossom must wither. A value system separated from its validation can survive only temporarily; after that, the best we can hope for is remnants and vestiges.

The communication between recent generations has been all too effective. The generation of Stage Two conveyed the message that while it cherished some of the effects and rewards of Jewishness, being Jewish has no substantial meaning. As a result, by Stage Three, the rewards and beauties, the sentiments and memories of Judaism, were already absent, and the Stage Three generation has no qualms about extending the challenge and indifference from the authority behind the values to the values themselves.

This, I propose is what Jewish parents, teachers, and communities must face if they are concerned about Jewish survival in America: the *fruits* of Judaism are delicious, but it is the *roots* of Judaism that give them life. The rewards of Judaism are delightful, but unless we see them within the total context of our faith, we will not be able to enjoy them. If Jewishness is to survive, it can do so only on the basis of Torah, the bond between G-d and man. The sterility of alternatives has been demonstrated at the cost of too many young lives.

The Changing Morality

(Remarks before a convention of the Lubavitcher Women's Organization)

A salient characteristic of *Chabad* is its method of penetrating beneath the surface, its stress on going beyond the obvious, its drive to the core of things. *Etzem*, essence, is a common *Chabad* term defined exhaustively in *Chabad* literature, because it describes the true, the "essential" nature of the subject at hand. Whether discussing the nature of man, the significance of an experience, the meaning of a Biblical passage, or attempting to reconcile disparate interpretations of G-d's essence, the recognition of *etzem* makes for a new understanding.

Let us apply something of this approach of seeking out *etzem* to the famous "Changing Morality," and the equally famous, or notorious, "Generation gap" as an extension of the "Three Stages." The subject is urgent enough to warrant further discussion, and—who knows?—perhaps even action. We may repeat a thought the late Rebbe, of blessed memory, expressed, and apply it here.

The Gemara speaks of the "craftiness" of the *yetzer ha-ra,* the evil impulse that urges man to sin. The *yetzer ha-ra* does not push man into sin all at once. "Today it tells a man, 'Do this,' and tomorrow it tells him, 'Do that,' until finally it tells him, 'Now go and worship idols.' " The *yetzer ha-ra* begins by telling a man to commit what he may consider a "minor" transgression, something trivial. Next, it induces him to proceed to a graver transgression and so on until he has sunk to the level of paganism.

The late Lubavitcher Rebbe gave a novel interpretation to this Gemara. The *yetzer ha-ra*, he tells us, does not necessarily tell a man to sin. In fact, he might urge man to do one *mitzvah* today, another *mitzvah* tomorrow, and to keep on performing *mitzvot*. Yet, the end result will be "idol-worship," utter evil, for the *yetzer ha-ra* wants man to do the *mitzvah* all for the wrong reasons. Man is to perform the *mitzvah* because he, the man, approves of it, because he agrees that the *mitzvah* makes sense to him—in short, for every conceivable reason except the proper one, which is simply that it is a *mitzvah* given by G-d. The "craftiness" of the *yetzer ha-ra* lies in its shrewd insight into man persuading man that nothing stands higher than himself, that he alone ultimately decides the validity of any idea, any code, any discipline, and that he is the sole arbiter when it comes to questions of ethics and morality. Perform any *mitzvah* you like, the evil impulse whispers, but only because it meets with your approval, not because it is a Divine commandment.

May I suggest that there is no generation gap at all, that, in essence, there also is no such thing as a "changing morality," but that what we are witnessing today is the natural and inevitable result of a process initiated some time ago. Seeds are planted, and eventually trees grow from them. The one who first planted the seed may not have realized what the result would be. He might be disappointed when he sees the tree, but the fact remains that it was he who planted the seed and that the tree is therefore the result of his work. In the same manner, parents instill in their offspring certain attitudes and values. The resulting "tree" might horrify the parents, but the children did not break with their parents; they only acted in accordance with the values they had been taught, the "seed."

We can compare one moral code, or value system with others and note their differences. However, the fundamental issue of the "changing morality," as this generation knows it, is not *which* morality, *which* code, or *which* values to accept, but ultimately whether *any* moral code should be accepted at all. Must man be "moral"? Is there any firm moral code that can be set down for all to observe?

Let me illustrate my point. Social scientists point out that moral codes vary from society to society. Polygamy is prohibited generally; yet, certain primitive cultures still permit the practice. We need only think of the lives of our own forefathers and remember that polygamy was not expressly banned until the edict of Rabbenu Gershom*—and all this was considered as being within Torah Judaism. At any rate, polygamy is an example of variations in definitions of "right" and "wrong."

The problem with which we are faced today is to determine whether "absolutes" such as "right" and "wrong" exist at all. Do as I myself have done on more than one occasion: challenge a group of students to suggest a given act that is wrong. You might expect them to answer categorically that it is wrong to kill or to steal, but this is the answer you will not get.

You will be given a vigorous argument, not perhaps, to justify murder or robbery, but that there is no logical imperative to condemn these acts. Whatever a society prohibits, you will be assured, is wrong for that society, but this does mean that it is intrinsically wrong.*

Cannibals, you will be told by the earnest young scholars, eat their victims, Eskimos kill their aged, and ancient Spartans put the feeble out to die. Each of these practices, we are informed, is "moral" for that particular society. Of course, none of this is new, but I suggest that a new critical change in attitude has emerged. Primitive savagery was regarded in the past as an evil that civilized man has outgrown. Barbarism was never considered justifiable, it was a reminder of the lowly origins of man and society. Today such conduct is no longer regarded as a vestige from a less humane past. It is blandly inappropriate to today's society, in the eyes of the contemporary, a *faux pas*, but it is not

---

*R. Gershom ben Judah (965-1028) who was active in Mayence, Germany. His other laws included prohibitions against: divorcing a woman without her consent, reading letters addressed to others, and mocking apostates who had returned to Judaism.

*For a discussion of man's inability to define good and evil, see the essay, "Good, Evil and Intellect".

condemned as gross immorality. Indeed, we are informed, given another set of circumstances, such behavior might be regarded as acceptable and even proper.

Here is the fruit of the seed planted by the older generation: the questioning—or outright rejection—of moral imperatives as such. Again, it is not a question of *which* morality to reject, but whether *any* morality should be accepted at all.

I can hear the indignant retort. How dare you imply that the moral problems we are facing today are the inevitable flowering of "seeds" planted by parents! To say that the past generation was immoral, or encouraged amorality or rejected morality, would be unjustifiably harsh criticism.

Permit me to make a sweeping generalization here: in making moral decisions today, American Jews do not use the classic moral standards. The historical Jewish standard—and this too is a generalization—was, "Is this permitted or not?" If it is not permitted, the discussion, and problem, ended right there. It was "out," period. If Torah does *not* prohibit an act, then one may go on to decide for himself. But the basic consideration was whether or not the act was in accordance with Torah.

Today—and this may refer to American Jewry for the last century—the standard is not what the Torah requires, but what is "done" or "not done" by others. If "everybody" does something, it is acceptable; if "it isn't done" one would be foolhardy to defy society. Take any moral decision, vital or trivial. Here, a word on fashion, on *tzniut,* on modesty and dignity in dress (and for that matter, in speech and comportment too), is in order. There is no thought about what the fashion or fad really represents, what caused it, and how it can affect its followers. Clothes not only express the person, they also influence his attitudes, his feelings about himself and others and his conduct. (Use the feminine pronoun if you wish; it's all the same.)

At a recent convention of *Chabad* women, the Lubavitcher Rebbe pointed out references in as early a source as Chapter 3 of the Book of Isaiah to the lack of *tzniut,* of modesty in dress and conduct. So, the "changing morality" is nothing new; it is, in fact, several dozen centuries old. Talk about being "modern"! We have seen the horrors, as the Rebbe put is, what happens when *tzniut* is neglected. We need not spell out the details; the newspapers do that plainly enough. Tragedies that were once completely unknown in Jewish families have become almost commonplace today. *Tzniut,* modesty, on the other hand, the Zohar and Gemara tell us, brings blessings, both material and spiritual.

It must be made plain that young girls are being exploited today by fashion arbiters, misogynists who think of the girl's welfare last, if they do at all. So much of America's life-style is determined by people who are devoid of morals and character, but geniuses at garnering publicity, at popularizing every possible vulgarity.

The *Chumash* tells us not to bring any *to'eva,* "abomination," into our homes. Even the newspaper ads are— pardon my Philistinism—dirty. Popular family-type magazines, journals devoted to "news," are abomination, to judge by their articles and photographs. Don't protest that these journals are merely telling it "like it is"—they are making it what it is. They don't *report* news—they *make* news. Publicity is the life blood of the "Beautiful People" (what a revolting misnomer) and their "New Morality." Without TV and printed publicity they would never have been able to acquire the influence they are wielding today. These are the people who are making decisions for us today with regard to our clothing, our reading, our entertainment, our art—in short, our lives.

We can find plenty of evidence of the new standard for decision-making. I recall talking to a fine young citizen of my community about sending his son to a Jewish day school. The question of *chinuch* (Jewish education) did not arise, the academic standards of the school were irrelevant, the Jewish and human development of the child did not matter. The decision hinged on one factor: if "everybody" sent their children, he said, then he would too. He abdicated his responsibility as a father, he denied himself the freedom of decision as a free man in a free country, in order to follow the crowd.

The message that parents are communicating to their children today is clear and strong. "When you make your decisions, don't look to the Torah, just look around you and see what people do today." "People" are a nameless, faceless entity, but "they" are supposed to be the ones to tell you how to educate your children, how to dress, what entertainment to enjoy, how to live. I submit that there is no gap between parents and children at all. They are both agreed that such concepts as "principle," "right," "decency" and "Judaism" count for very little. The only difference between the generations is that parents and children don't follow the same "thems."

Old and young alike feel that the only criteria for life are whatever is "popular," "acceptable," and "fashionable." But, unhappily for the parents who repudiated *Shabbos* and *kashrut* because these things did not count in the circles in which *they* moved, their children have carried the principle of "following the crowd" into their own lives. And since they live in a world where gross immorality is more than acceptable, they go along with the present day trend. If "society" condones the use of narcotics by the young, who would dare defy society? After all, this is what their parents explicitly taught them, "Don't be different."

The young are left with a heritage of aimlessness, of lack of direction because they were never given any firm standards to follow. But they are not satisfied with the pap they were fed. They are thirsty for thoughts, challenges, ideals. They are our spiritually underprivileged, the Jewishly deprived. Their apparently bizarre choices of life-style testify to their desperation, their vulnerability to fads and manipulation.

There is challenge here for everyone, and responsibility—for parents, for teachers, for rabbis, for every member of the community—to teach and demonstrate what a life of Jewish substance can be.

The Uses of Torah

I am frequently asked why we should turn to an ancient code of laws for guidance. Are our human instincts of elemental justice not adequate guides? This question has been troubling a great many Jews and made them uncertain in their commitment to Judaism. What is the relevance of Torah to life in our own day?

The problem is that often the Torah is used for a variety of purposes which in fact are irrelevant to it, while its primary function and objective, its ultimate *raison d'etre*, has been obscured and overlooked. In recent times, Torah has been subjected to a "refinement" of purpose; this means that the irrelevancies have been relegated to their proper, peripheral sphere, and the areas where Torah is forever indispensable have been clarified.

Let us cite the areas in which the Torah has become "irrelevant." Reading the Hebrew Bible, we encounter history and narrative, poetry, biographies of individuals and the history of mankind. For thousands of years the Torah provided its followers with drama, literature, and a sense of history and continuity when these were hardly obtainable from any other source. But contemporary man, curious about his origins and antecedents, has access to an ever-expanding array of sources for this purpose. Archeology literally and figuratively uncovers the secrets of yesterday. The tools of the anthropologist and the historian provide material for those interested in knowledge of the past. As a result, the functions of the Torah as a source book for the history of mankind has become an anachronism.

Before the advent of science, man's environment and the

processes of nature were shrouded in mystery. Natural phenomena were regarded as supernatural, beyond the understanding and certainly beyond the control of mortals. The weather, disease, earthquakes were considered tò be beyond man's ken. Only "religion"—the appeal to powers transcending those of mere men—could "explain" good fortune or calamity. Religion provided a framework that gave some meaning to an unfathomable world. But obviously, contemporary man no longer looks to "religion"— construed in this sense—for such enlightenment. Science, to use an inclusive term, has successfully assumed the function of explaining the processes of nature.

We could go on enumerating areas where formerly man looked to religion (or Torah) for guidance: concepts like civil legislation and quarantine for infectious diseases gained currency—if they did not originate—in Torah.

But in our day man's own resources are sufficient for all those needs. He no longer needs to turn to revelation. In fact, he spurns the very suggestion because his own competence has become so vast. Having invented the sciences, he can speculate plausibly on the origin of the cosmos. He can find cures for deadly diseases and feels he can arrange his society with its economic and legal systems quite by himself, thank you, without reference to the supernatural. To present the Bible today as a guidebook for those aspects of practical life would be to make the Bible a redundancy and worse.

Interestingly, there is one area of Torah teaching that has always been regarded as within man's grasp: the laws of morality. The social laws contained in the Torah were considered as self-evident moral truths—stealing and murder are indisputably evil—and the only question was why the Torah should bother with things that were so obvious. Good and evil, right and wrong have become part of the universal lexicon. We might quibble about trivia, about fine points of definition, but the basic validity and the broad application of these are beyond challenge.

But even as man's scientific competence expanded so

fabulously, it also found its limitations. In its own framework, it is potentially infinite. Observable phenomena and measurable quantities are raw material for the scientist—or for man, if you will. But before long, it became evident that there are "things" which are not readily observable or subject to quantitative measurement. The scientist could deal with "what" happens, and "how," but the "why" was beyond his purview. Right and wrong could not be tested, observed or measured by any of his instruments, not even the philosopher's intellect. The scientist therefore concluded that as a *scientist* he was in no position to make "value judgments." For him as a scientist there is no such thing as "good" or "evil."

Values persist, moral decisions continue to be made (even if negatively, through default), but neither the scientist's laboratory nor the philosopher's seminar offer guidance here. The scientist can explain how a heart is transplanted or how an atom bomb can be exploded, but he cannot tell us whether, morally, we are justified in doing these things. Today's secular philosopher does not concern himself with the classic problems of good and evil, not because he is indifferent, or because he feels that these problems have been resolved, but because his philosopher's tools are inadequate or inappropriate to the task. These particular concepts are outside his realm. In other words, man does not possess the *human* resources to define or even justify morality as morality. Unhappily, the problem of morality remains, for, aside from being a scientist, the scientist may also be a father, and he will hardly be ready to rear his children without these concepts of decency and humanity, even if the most sophisticated computer cannot deal with them. We do want our children to be honest and clean.

The concepts of "good" and "moral" must be recognized as distinct from "prudent" and "effective." Whatever they might describe, and whatever appeal they might possess, the latter terms do not entail "morality." It may be "prudent" to be honest. But there may be circumstances where "prudence" might conceivably prescribe larceny.

As so many erstwhile physical truths came under the scrutiny of the challenge, "Is it true?"—the challenge was extended to moral truths as well. Remember, revelation has been repudiated by the secularist and Scripture cannot "justify" its moral statements for him. Why, then, under safe circumstances, should we not steal? Since mores—and morals—are so commonly ascribed to the societies in which they are observed, if "society" can determine morals, what shall we make of an Adolf Eichmann, whom Nazi society considered a paragon of virtue? Shall consensus indeed determine morality? Wouldn't this mean that anything is proper as long as "everybody does it"? And if this is so, which "society's" dictates am I bound to observe—those of the hippies or those of the Babbitts? And, granted that violations of these dictates may be highly "imprudent," are these violations "immoral"?

Here Torah comes into its own. Man's resources are indeed inadequate, but he is not limited to human resources. Today we turn to revelation, to the "supernatural," if you insist, not for explanations of the why's of a drought, but for guidance on how to live. We could not know that on our own. Man was able logically, rationally, and scientifically, to build a Nazi Germany.

Whatever history or narrative, biography or poetry, there is in Torah, their purpose, no less than that of the mitzvot and prohibitions contained in the Torah, is to instruct man. If, in the process, we also learn about some Egyptian dynasty, or Near Eastern pre-history, fine. But this is not the intention and purpose of the Torah. Its objective is solely to teach us how to live.

This is the "refinement of purpose" to which the Torah has been subjected: man's heightened awareness of the communication between the Divine and the mortal. Torah is a work of instruction and guidance. Its purpose is to show man the superhuman element that dwells within him, to make him aware of his human potential—in short, to teach him how to conduct his life.

Emunah:
The Role
of Faith in Judaism

The problem of faith has returned to torment so many who had been certain of their immunity to such concerns. They are no longer secure in their lack of religious belief; they are disturbed by a nagging half-belief, as it were. What upset their composure, their rather cavalier dismissal of religious faith?

Perhaps it was disillusionment with faiths other than religious, the political or economic panaceas which they had thought would bring about a brave new world. The militant non-faiths of an earlier generation have proven illusory. Man has come to realize that he will probably never be able to plumb the mysteries that only yesterday seemed all but in his grasp. Quests for Nirvana have turned out to be futile. The Jew in particular may have had dreams of some universal humanity transcending ancestry and nationality, a world in which he would be able cheerfully to abandon his Jewishness. But these dreams too have been shattered by harsh realities. Who can be blamed for being cynical today about the belief that man is capable of perfection?

Fortunately most Jews, whatever their station, accept their Jewishness. They are seeking an answer to the next question: How are they to give expression to their Jewishness? Virtually illiterate in the formal teachings of Judaism and totally unfamiliar with its practices, they explore—gingerly and tentatively—the treasure bequeathed to them by centuries and generations. *Mitzvot*? Torah? Tell me more about them! How do you use these *tefillin*, and may I do this or that on the Sabbath? I can't read Hebrew. How, then, am I to worship? And when these questions are answered to their satisfaction they pull themselves up short. "But wait a minute! What if I don't *believe* in all this?" Obviously, the question whether they *believe* in all this is a fundamental consideration which they feel they must resolve before they can proceed to *act* in good conscience, without feeling guilty of hypocrisy. The question of faith becomes a major obstacle to the Jew groping his way back. How can he move if he does not *"believe"*?

Our first task should be to place faith in its proper position in the hierarchy of *mitzvot*. This might be understood better by using contrast as well as direct description. The Western Jew—and obviously it is to him that we have been referring with all his Western-ness of culture, outlook, and values, and poverty in Jewish learning and living—has absorbed the surrounding culture, and accepts its unarticulated attitudes uncritically and unconsciously. He does this specifically in defining faith and judging its necessity.

To Western man, whether he be personally religious or atheist, what he calls "religion" is rooted in faith, if indeed it does not consist entirely of faith. The factor that sets apart the "religious" from the irreligious, is the critical question, "Do you believe?" His total religious experience is classed as valid or false, depending on how he answers this question. The Jew has tended to adapt this Western, non-Jewish approach to his own ancestral faith, and so when he examines the state of his belief, his acceptance of religious doctrine, he becomes alarmed. In the face of the challenge which he cannot answer—for he insists that he does *not* "believe"—he is ready to give up and try to find himself in a context outside of Judaism. This difficulty of apparent lack of faith may seem crucial to others, but it should really not be such a problem for the Jew.

Let us analyze some aspects of faith. The Talmud speaks of a burglar who offers a prayer before breaking into a house. If he prays, how can he be a thief? Conversely, if he is a thief, how can he find it in his heart to pray? We can, of course, simply dismiss the thief as a superficial hypocrite mouthing a meaningless formula. This will make us feel so pleasantly superior and "spiritual." But then we will also lose an opportunity for insight into ourselves and into the nature of faith itself.

Chabad literature categorizes some qualities as pervasive and others as peripheral. The pervasive qualities are the ones that make themselves felt, such as emotions that fill the heart or thoughts that occupy the mind. If one's deeds are not in character with one's thoughts and feelings, then there is something missing in his mind or his heart. If an inventor's idea looks feasible on the drawing-board but turns out to be impracticable in reality, then there must be something wrong with the idea. The validity of the thought is something that can be tested.

Faith, on the other hand, is a peripheral quality. If faith proves ineffective, this does not mean that it is invalid, or based on a lie. By its very nature, faith may exist on a plane separate from the thoughts, feelings, words and deeds of men, without any points of contact. There are people whose behavior is not in character with their professed beliefs. This means that such persons are not consistent, but it does not mean that the faith itself is necessarily illusory.

The Prophet says that the "righteous lives by his faith"; this is the hallmark of the saintly person. In such people there is no dichotomy between conviction and performance, and they are properly lauded as "righteous." The Talmud calls this passage from the Prophets the summation, the one all-encompassing statement of Torah. Others may place faith and life into two separate compartments, but the saint refuses to do so. Each phase of his life reflects his faith, and because his faith is pure and selfless, his life will be G-dly, too. It is interesting to note that the Prophet does not equate saintliness with faith, but with *living* by one's faith. (One can have faith, but not live by it, like our praying burglar.)

While only G-d can penetrate into the recesses of the soul to evaluate the sincerity of someone's faith, we may indulge in the temptation to sit in judgment on others for a moment. We have seen that a man's way of life may contradict the faith he professes. It could reasonably be argued that such a person's faith is deficient, that he is shallow or a hypocrite. Professed faith and true belief are not synonymous. But conversely, the mere professing of atheism is not necessarily identical with atheism.

On that unforgettable day in June, 1967, at the Wall, avowed atheists prayed and wept with the fervor of the truly devout. Atheists? This spark of faith that was uncovered under such dramatic circumstances may be an illustration of a point frequently made by the Alter Rebbe in his early *Chabad* works dealing with faith.

The Rebbe declared that every Jew is naturally endowed with faith as a heritage from his forebears, beginning with the Patriarchs. In the course of his life this spark may become eclipsed by other considerations. (The Lubavitcher Rebbe equates "uncovering faith" with "uncovering soul.") Man's situation in a mundane universe is not ideally suited to fan this spark so that it might blaze forth. The nearness of the Creator is not readily evident and the moral imperatives of His commands are blocked out by the temptations of the moment. It requires effort to fan the spark of faith. Man must call upon the internal resources of his soul to overcome his weakness. The naked eye sees only the delights of the moment and at such times Divine strictures seem vague and inconsequential. If man is to conduct himself as he should, he must enlist the aid of his faith.

This faith is inherent in him and can be aroused. However, this is not the epitome of faith. To understand this better, let us distinguish between faith and reason.

There are some areas where the intellect is competent, and others where it is irrelevant. Man and his mind are limited in time and space. We may use a term like "infinite," but we cannot conceive of true infiniteness, if only because our own personal existence impinges on Infinity.

If something is truly infinite, then how can we exist? (This, of course, is a classic problem of theology which is discussed in *Chabad* literature, but is is not our concern for the moment.) "Infinite" here is not the same as an "infinite number" that mathematicians use. It is absolute, countenancing no other existence, so there can be only one Infinite and nothing else can exist. "There is nothing else"—is repeated in the *Aleinu* prayer from the *Chumash*. We can conceive of the finite, however vast, and can expand our comprehension within these limits through study. Naturally, these limits will vary from person to person. But beyond finiteness reason is inoperative.

(Another area of faith is the undemonstrable—noted in the essay, "Revelation"—for example our faith in the coming of the *Moshiach*. Maimonides asserts this faith quite forcefully: "I believe with perfect faith . . . " *Moshiach* cannot be proven by demonstration or logic. He is accepted—or expected—as an act of faith. Note that faith does not contradict knowledge. The touted conflict between faith and reason is a chimera.)

However, man's inability to comprehend the infinite does not mean that infinity does not exist. Man is in fact capable of apprehending this state, but not through his mind. He can do this only through faith. Faith functions where reason cannot tread. We speak of the Infinite, but we can describe Him at most in negative terms—He is not limited, etc. What is this Infinite? We do not, can not, know. But we do believe that He is the ultimate in perfection, the truly unbounded, with no limitations or finiteness, transcending mind and understanding. Furthermore—and this is vital—we believe that Infinite G-d and tiny man communicate with each other, that He has revealed His will and His thoughts to man, and that He cares about man's life and hears man when he calls upon Him.

Let us return to our concerned Jew who wants Judaism, yet is disturbed by his inability to "believe." How can he overcome the handicap of unbelief? Faith is a mitzvah, a cardinal one to be sure, supreme perhaps, but it is only one

61

of 613 commandments, a peer among peers. To believe is one of the many mitzvot that we are required to observe. Belief is not the test of piety, nor is it a "first step" in Judaism. For others, faith might be the summation of their religion, or at least the indispensable first step. For the Jew, faith is not the beginning, but the reward of Torah living. In Judaism, one does not begin with faith; faith follows.

The Alter Rebbe wrote about the act of "nourishing faith," with "faith" being the object of the verb "nourishing." Faith requires nourishment, strengthening and cultivation. The Rebbe noted that Israel is by nature endowed with faith as its heritage, but he insisted that the Jew must progress far beyond this point. The *mitzvot*, he explained, are bound up with the Infinite, for they are His Will. By performing a *mitzvah* man is bound up with the Infinite. Through the *mitzvah* of Torah study man's mind coalesces with the "mind" of G-d; through *mitzvot* requiring speech his faculty of speech is joined to G-d's; through performing *mitzvot* of action, his power to act is combined with G-d's. The performance of *mitzvot* brings the reality of G-d within the reach of man. The transcendent G-d, beyond all apprehension, illuminates man's soul. He is not distant to man, nor indifferent to insignificant mortals. Does man now understand G-d? His mind is as limited as before, but he apprehends G-d through his faculty of faith as he could not have done before.

Another observation on faith. I find the common pejorative "blind faith" a mindless tautology. What would be a "seeing" faith, presumably the acceptable form, or "understandable" faith? If an idea is obvious or understandable, who needs faith? If the validity of an idea cannot be demonstrated and proven, isn't its acceptance an act of "blind" faith? The pejorative implication of the term "blind faith" is that faith is tantamount to ignorance, an escape from the rigors of thinking. But the heretic is not, I regret to say, more vigorous intellectually than the believer. The believer knows everything that the heretic knows, but he is not at an impasse. He does not accept the limitations of intellect as limitations on man's striving. When the believer finds that the mind's instruments are unavailing, he turns to some other human resource for guidance and for the answers that reason cannot seem to provide. And the resource to which he turns is—faith.

Between Challenge and Response:
Notes on a Function of Faith

There is a certain element of faith that has played a crucial role throughout Jewish history, quite apart from the more conventional function of faith, accepting that which defies proof or understanding. If one cannot prove the existence of G-d, he may accept Him on faith. If one cannot demonstrate the Divine origin of the Torah, he may accept the premise of revelation on faith. Such are the conventional functions of faith. Faith functions in areas that are inaccessible to human reason.

But there is one element in faith that has served to secure the survival of the Jewish people through the ages: the firm conviction that there is an answer for every challenge that we may be called upon to meet. Throughout its history, Israel has had to contend with such challenges, spiritual and ideological. Let us examine some.

The Idolatry of the Canaanites: Modern minds wonder why so much attention should be paid to idolatry. Paganism, after all, is a primitive, outlandish thing, long dead. Does the Second Commandment, "You shall have no other gods before Me" still have relevance today? Maybe it does. Idolatry is putting one's faith in tangibles, in power, wealth, in things we can see and touch. Without reading unwarranted sophistication into the ancients' crude conceptions of deities, we suggest that today's generation has not progressed radically from that primitive stage except perhaps verbally. Down through the ages, the idols of man have hardly changed form. Golden calves are still worshipped.

The upsurge of a neo-paganism, short-lived we pray, drawing on Eastern cults, verges on ancient idolatry.

The Insitution of Monarchy: Eventually, in the Land of Israel, the leadership of the people was transferred from the prophets to the "secular power," which was represented by a king. The ideals of king and prophet were not always in agreement with one another. Innate human weakness, the individual's susceptibility to temptation, was now coupled with the personal ambitions and weaknesses of the monarch. Immorality was institutionalized, while the prophets became objects of scorn, with few listening.

The Destruction of the First Sanctuary: The Holy City Jerusalem and the Sanctuary represented G-d's presence among the people of Israel. No matter how gravely Israel had sinned, the L-rd had remained in its midst. Suddenly, the Jews saw the "dwelling-place" of G-d go up in flames. This catastrophe shattered the Jew's image of his whole world. The hub was gone—could there be any future?

The Babylonian Exile: By the time the Babylonians drove the Jews into exile, the Kingdom of Israel—the ten tribes which represented the majority of the Jewish people—had long vanished. What hope was there for the two weak tribes of Judah to survive? Jerusalem the capital had been plowed under, and no two stones of the spiritual center, the Sanctuary, had remained together.

Persian Tolerance: The familar story of Purim can be a paradigm for the blandishments of assimilation, followed by the eruption of latent Jew-hatred, that have been such frequent phenomena in recent Jewish history.

Hellenism: This was not a challenge of brute force but one of ideology, and one by no means unattractive at that. We have had parallels aplenty in periods of history closer to our own day. There is Western culture with its science, literature and philosophy. The Jews of the ghettoes in Poland and Russia two hundred years ago could afford to look with indifference upon the cultural level of the Gentiles who surrounded them, but the Jews of 19th-century France and Germany—like their ancestors in Maccabaean

Judea—could not so easily dismiss the culture of their Gentile neighbors as inferior to their own. The beauty of ancient Greece—Noah's son Yaphet was traditionally identified with the charms of Greek antiquity—could not be disparaged. The conflict between Athens and Jerusalem was not a clash of armies; it was a struggle between spirits and intellects. The smart and fashionable Jews of the Hellenist era went to the gymnasium, to the theater and to the circus, not to the humble, unimpressive house of study. Some of the most prominent Jewish leaders of the day were Hellenists. Hellenism seemed to represent the wave of the future. Only backward people, it appeared, could prefer the outdated ways of Judaism to the ideas of the forward-looking Greeks.

The Sadducees: So-called "interpretations" or "wings" of Judaism are not modern inventions, and deviations did not always present themselves as opponents of tradition. Sadducees by any name, and particularly when associated with wealth, social prestige and political power, pose formidable threats to Jewish survival. Incidentally, every Jew alive today is descended not from the Sadducees but from the Pharisees, who represent the mainstream of tradition. The others either eventually returned to that mainstream, or else were lost to Judaism. "Pharisee," by the way, is a term of high praise in Judaism . . .

Rome and the Second Destruction of Jerusalem: The survival of the Jewish people after the Roman conquest of Jerusalem was assured by a rabbi, R. Yohanan ben Zakkai, and his instrument for the preservation of Judaism was—a yeshiva, the Torah school in Yavne. Who were the political leaders of the Jewish people during that critical era? Except for historians, few people know. But everyone knows Rabbi Akiva. Our earlier exiles in Egypt and Babylonia were relatively brief. But our Roman exile has continued some 2,000 years. How was it possible for a people to endure such a long exile from its homeland, quite apart from the incredible persecutions which it suffered throughout that exile?

Christianity, Islam, the Crusades, and the Inquisition: These and their modern-day equivalents are familiar and continuous challenges to Jewish survival.

The Industrial Revolution: Changing social and economic conditions of necessity affected the quality of Jewish religious life. The total re-ordering of society was reflected in the Jewish world. Again, an unprecedented challenge. No institution survived unscathed. Would Judaism survive?

"Emancipation" and the breakdown of the European ghettoes, America with its unprecedented opportunities, the rise of Socialism, the revolutions that have been with us over the past two centuries, and that ultimate horror, the Nazi Holocaust, are only a few examples of more recent challenges that have threatened the survival of Judaism. Quite a list.

The fact that we are still living as Jews today is evidence that each of these challenges evoked a strong response. Other peoples, the cultures and empires of antiquity, were lost because they could not cope with threats to their existence, but the Jewish people were different. The Jews have always managed to respond in a manner that ensured their survival.

The Lubavitcher Rebbe once explained the phenomenon of Jewish survival to a convention of Chabad women. He based his discourse on the insitution of *Sh'mittah* (the Sabbatical Year), which, Torah emphasizes, was given to Israel *on Mount Sinai. Sh'mittah,* the Rebbe pointed out, affords a symbol of the staying power of the Jewish people.

The cultures of the other nations were relevant only to the times and circumstances under which they emerged and flourished. They could not cope with history's inexorably changing circumstances and therefore, notwithstanding their initial wealth and power, eventually became obsolete and vanished.

Not so the Jewish people. Their ability to withstand the shifts of changing conditions is symbolized by the *Sh'mittah* year. The period of *Sh'mittah* extends over the full cycle of all the four seasons—the bitter cold of winter, the torrid

67

heat of summer, the promise of spring and the decline of autumn. *Sh'mittah* endures through periods of flowering and of decay. *Sh'mittah* is explicitly linked to Sinai, to Torah, for Torah endures through the ages, transcending all the upheavals of history. The survival of Israel is not dependent on particular circumstances. It finds effective responses to challenges from without by seeking in Torah.

When the first Sanctuary was destroyed by the Babylonians, the Jews, to put it in homely terms, set up *shuls* and began to *daven*. Israel was preserved by the little *siddur*. Torah scholars arose to replace the political leadership, and the second destruction of Jerusalem was followed by the emergence of a "portable Sanctuary" in the form of the Yeshiva, or Talmud academy.

The Talmud and, when mastery of the entire Talmud became too formidable a task, the great Codes of Jewish Law, represented Judaism's response to the need for making the Torah accessible to all Jews. In more recent times *Chassidus* in Poland, the Mussar movement in Lithuania, and Hirschian Orthodoxy in Germany all were responses to new crises that endangered Jewish survival.

However, in some instances, there was a time gap between the challenge and the response. Thus, false Messiahs and horrible pogroms took a severe toll in Poland years before the appearance of the Baal Shem Tov, and assimilation was rampant in 19th-century Germany for some time before the emergence of S.R. Hirsch's philosophy of *Torah Im Derkh Eretz.*

We suggest that the bridging of this gap between challenge and response was a *function of faith.* We are faced with a problem; at the first moment, we have no ready answer, but we firmly declare, "I know that there is an answer, and that eventually we will find it." In the end, the answers were always forthcoming, but often too many of us were lost before the answers materialized.

Thus, Socialism was touted in 19th-century Russia as a panacea for the ills of the persecuted Jewish people. Forget about religion, the "opiate of the masses." Equal rights and equal opportunities, it was said, would bring about the full integration of the Jews. An independent Jewish homeland would eliminate marginality and anti-Semitism. Marx and Darwin, humanism and secularism all presented formidable challenges in their day. From our present vantage point, we might wonder how the Jews could have failed to see the flaws of these Utopian promises, but at the time their blandishments were real threats to Jewish survival. We have not yet fully recovered from them. The response is already here, but not everyone perceives it.

It takes faith to confront these challenges with confidence in our position even when we cannot provide immediate answers to every question. It is this function of faith that has persevered Israel.

But isn't this an exaggeration? It never took centuries to develop our responses to a given crisis. Couldn't Israel have survived even without that faith? After all, what is one single generation in a history of over 150 generations, spanning thousands of years?

Here, we must remember that any tradition is only one generation old. One hundred and fifty generations can build up a tradition, but if Generation 151 is not taught, and the chain is broken, there will be no 152nd. Every generation therefore has the duty to preserve and transmit its heritage from the past, because the neglect of only one generation can wipe out thousands of years of work and sacrifice.

Perhaps Generation 151 does not have the answers, but if it has faith that the answers exist somewhere, and are only waiting to be brought forth, we may be certain that Generation 152 will be there to produce the answer.

Jewish Commitment and Free Inquiry

"*Chabad*—or better, Judaism— insists on faith and on the acceptance of certain concepts," a scientist observed at an Encounter, "but how can I reconcile that with my personal need for free inquiry? In my profession, I must be free to examine all presuppositions. I should not have to accept them simply because someone else tells me that I must."

First, a word about the place of questioning and challenging in the Torah. Torah is meant to be understood; in fact, it is a *mitzvah* to understand the Word of G-d. If you do not understand what the Torah says, you are not fulfilling the *mitzvah* of Torah knowledge. Indeed, as the Rebbe once explained in discussing hippies, the Torah *requires* us to challenge, to question.

However, the Rebbe also added a key concept: the challenge should be stated, but one's observance of the law or precept in question must not be made dependent on whether the response one receives is considered "satisfactory." It is not acceptable in Judaism to say, "All right, I'll observe the Sabbath if you can give me an explanation I can accept." Chabad teaches us to recognize man's intellectual powers, but also the limitations of these powers. Let's be specific.

In every problem there is scope for inquiry, but there are also *a priori* statements. Thus, in studying the family, we have such statements as the Seventh Commandment, "You shall not commit adultery," the Fifth Commandment, "Honor your father and your mother," and the commandment in Deuteronomy 6, "You shall teach them diligently to your children." Here we have representative obligations that are part of the relationship between husband and wife, parents and children—obligations which, by the way, flow in both directions.

It is our duty to strive to understand these three precepts, but on no account may we hold our observance in abeyance until we have received what we consider an adequate rationalization for them. Here, inquiry must be confined to abstract, intellectual attempts at comprehension.

Then there are practical forms that inquiry may take: which is better, the nuclear family, or the extended family? Go to it; you are free to discuss the subject in detail. Is the kibbutz method of child-rearing superior to the more conventional way? Study the question; examine relevant data, but note always that the basic assumptions of Torah remain undisturbed. Your kibbutz may serve as a surrogate for parents, if you wish, but the parents remain responsible for the child's upbringing. No matter how they do it, it is still their responsibility to see to it that their children are "taught diligently."

Or take fidelity between husband and wife or the honor due one's parents. These are non-negotiable commandments. Someone may claim he is not convinced that marital faithfulness is the "best" way of life, or he may insist that he does not understand why he should observe the Seventh Commandment. However, this does not give him any justification in violating the Biblical ban on adultery. These are unequivocal commands set forth in the Torah. (Of course, these are only two examples; however, the principle is applicable to all of Jewish law.) Intellectual freedom, we may suggest, is unimpaired though other "freedoms" are radically restricted.

Now you may protest against all this. Shouldn't understanding, intellectual acceptance, be the prerequisite for observance? The challenge here is *not* to the idea that practice should precede comprehension, but to the idea of accepting a code that is "non-negotiable."

At the outset, we must recognize that the human intellect

is fallible. Human knowledge is by definition imperfect and in a perpetual state of flux. We cannot commit ourselves—to the point of discipline, hardship and sacrifice—to a concept that is tentative and subject to modification. We cannot have principled lives or make crucial decisions on the basis of statements founded on intellectual premises, because these premises are constantly subject to change.

Only in certain areas within the sphere of intellect can there be universal agreement: in the observable, the quantitative, the demonstrable, the objective—and even in these areas controversy is not unknown. But when it comes to such abstract matters as morality and spiritual values, intellectual consensus is virtually impossible, certainly as a guide for action. In areas where variations are the norm, where all variants are equally valid according to the standards of the intellect, no one pattern of behavior can be described as preferable to any other. We cannot, then, look to intellect for guidance. Intellect has certain spheres of competence in which it reigns supreme, but it is irrelevant in the moral sphere. (See "Good, Evil, and Intellect.")

Nor can we hold moral decisions in abeyance. If I postpone putting on *tefillin* until I understand the reason for that commandment, I am not "suspending judgment"; I have simply made a decision not to put on *tefillin* today. If I defer my decision to be a faithful spouse—or a respectful son or daughter—until I get a satisfactory explanation for the ban against adultery or for the commandment to honor my parents, I have not postponed making my decision but have already chosen my course, either deliberately or by forfeit.

The Torah's code of morality, its definitions of ethics, of right and wrong, are not necessarily ineluctable conclusions of reasoning. Some of them may not be readily supportable by sheer logic. But the laws of the Torah are *mitzvot* and the meaning of *mitzvah* is "commandment," binding and valid even when we cannot explain them.

In the areas of *mitzvot*, then, speculation cannot be the basis for choosing one's patterns of conduct, for speculation is incompetent in that sphere. It is merely an intellectual exercise. However, when it is engaged in, not as an independent function for the purpose of choosing one's way of life, but with the intent of exploring the meaning of the word of G-d, it will illuminate and enrich our religious observance. In this sense, Torah encourages, indeed demands, critical thinking. Quite apart from the requirements of Torah learning, we are to use our minds in every *mitzvah*, because our understanding of the *mitzvot* can generate enthusiasm in place of mechanical routine in their performance.

However, one's patterns of conduct cannot be based on subjective factors (anyone can find adequate intellectual justification for anything he passionately desires to do at a given moment), or on transitory considerations (for "new moralities" are constantly replaced by "newer" ones, and situational ethics are about as firm as quicksilver), or on what is socially acceptable (for what abomination was not acceptable to one "society" or another?).

But what of the *mitzvot* that we can consider "intellectually acceptable"? What does *Chabad* have to say about the function of intellect there?

In this connection, let us refer to the essay, "The Changing Morality," to the interpretation given by the late Rebbe to the Talmudic statement: "The *yetzer ha-ra* (evil impulse) within man is crafty. Today it tells a man, 'Do this,' and tomorrow it tells him, 'Do that,' until finally it tells him, 'Now go and worship idols.' " This, the Rebbe said, means to tell us that the corruption of the individual is not a sudden, dramatic, radical development. The process may be slow, so gradual as to be almost imperceptible. The *yetzer ha-ra* may not even tell a man to do evil. It might, in fact, tell him to perform good deeds—but for the wrong reasons. Do good, it may urge, because it is meaningful to *you*, because the idea meets with *your* approval. That it happens to be G-d's command is irrelevant. In this manner man, not G-d, is made the final arbiter of good and evil. And if man is qualified to accept certain values, he has the ability to reject them as well, if he so chooses. The tragic element here is that man's concept of what is "good" and "meaningful" is not constant. Yesterday's abomination is tolerable today and may even be considered a virtue tomorrow.

It was in order to emphasize this inadequacy of reason that the Torah has given us certain laws which are classed as *Chukkim*—statutes which defy intellectual understanding, which exceed the limits of the rational (the ban on eating swine, or the wearing of garments containing mixtures of wool and linen are familiar examples). The Torah also contains other categories of laws—*mishpatim*, ordinances of justice, "logical" laws to which the mind readily assents. But in order to teach man that his mind's assent to the word of G-d is redundant (he must *understand*, but whether or not he "agrees" with precept in question is irrelevant), the Torah inserted the *chukkim*. Even when man does not happen to understand a *mitzvah*, it is still a *mitzvah* to be obeyed. Conversely, when man does understand the *mitzvah*, the imperative to fulfull it comes not from the fact that he understands it, but from the source of the *mitzvah*—G-d Himself.

(The three types of *mitzvot* are explained in the essay "Mitzvot and Their Meaning.")

Miracles

A reply to a student's question at an Encounter

Why don't miracles happen any more?

Miracles—the word itself is hazy. Just what is a miracle? A world-shocking event such as the parting of the Red Sea at the time of the Exodus? Or the constant human act of breathing? Neither of these two phenomena can truly be explained, but one of them is a familiar, ongoing occurrence while the other is an exotic, one-time happening. Let's talk about miracles for a few moments and see whether miracles have really ceased.

The greatest miracle of all is described in the opening words of the Book of Genesis: "In the beginning, G-d created . . . " Suddenly "nothing" was transformed into "something." We are all familiar with the transformation of matter into energy or of energy into matter, but each of these changes involved a previously existing "something." Where "nothing" exists, there can be no change. Creating *ex nihilo*—literally, "out of nothing"—is beyond man's capabilities. This is a hurdle of acceptance that must be confronted at the outset. G-d, and G-d alone, can *create*. The miracle of creation is *the* miracle of the first order, beyond duplication by man.

The more familiar miracles described elsewhere in the Torah—the parting of the Red Sea, the *manna* in the wilderness, the light that burned in the Sanctuary for eight days (the miracle of Chanukah), and so forth—these are all miracles of the second order. They did not entail creation *ex nihilo*, but merely change. Water, which is liquid, suddenly behaves like a solid; this, in brief, is what happened when the Red Sea was parted to enable Israel to pass through it on dry land. A quantity of oil which normally can burn for only one day burns for eight full days because its rate of combustion has been slowed to one-eighth the ordinary rate. This, in brief, is the story of Chanukah. As the Talmud puts it, "He Who ordered oil to burn, and it burns, will order vinegar to burn and it, too, will burn."

But there is yet a third order of miracles—the miracles that are with us every day of our lives. The Sages teach us to "praise Him for every breath we draw." We are to give thanks to G-d for our every heartbeat, for the smooth performance of all our vital functions, and indeed for all the day-by-day workings of nature. "But," I hear someone protest, "that's only nature!" Correct. But the ordinary, the "natural," the everyday and commonplace happenings in nature and in our bodies are no less the work of G-d's hand than the parting of the Red Sea and, for that matter, the act of Creation itself. Thus we see that miracles are indeed still taking place and, in fact, are happening all the time.

This, by the way, is the explanation of the miracle of Purim, the deliverance of the Jewish people from Haman's wicked scheming: a succession of events which are not in themselves "supernatural," a series of what appears to be mere "coincidences" but which comes about at a time when it can do, and does, the most good.

The Lubavitcher Rebbe once compared the Torah perspective and the non-Torah (we might call it, the "scientific") perspective succinctly: the Torah view seeks the supernatural in the natural; science seeks the natural in the supernatural.

The function of the scientist is to find reasons for all the phenomena of nature, and then to apply his findings to all the natural events he subsequently encounters. He sets out from the premise that there is a reason for everything; he has faith in cause and effect. If an apparently healthy man suddenly falls sick and dies, the scientist cannot simply attribute it to the inscrutable will of G-d. His job is to find the cause of that illness, perhaps to cure others stricken with a similar disease, or perhaps to prevent the disease from striking others. Let it be emphasized that all this, in itself, is perfectly consonant with Torah doctrine. What are the physical causes of thunder and lightning, of rainbows, floods, earthquakes, eclipses and famines—indeed, of anything in the universe? An occurrence that seems to defy explanation simply presents that much more of a challenge. "At the present stage in our knowledge we cannot adequately explain this phenomenon," the scientist will note. But the fact remains that, as a scientist, he *must* find a "natural" explanation for whatever happens in the world in which we live.

Torah imparts a different perspective. From the vantage point of Torah, everything is "supernatural"—including nature. Nature itself is a miracle, created by the hand of G-d; without His charge, "Let there be . . . " it would have remained nothingness. Do your lungs work properly? If so, give thanks to G-d for that. The natural functions of your body have concealed within them the hand of G-d; without Him, they would not continue. That tree and that sunset are not just a beautiful tree and a glorious sunset; they are the manifestation of G-d Himself through His creations.

These two perspectives, science and Torah, are, of course, not mutually exclusive. The physician who is a Torah Jew will use all his professional skill to treat his patient, and yet remain sufficiently humble to recite some *Tehillim* (Psalms) as well. Or, we might express the same thought in the reverse; the Torah Jew who is a physician will offer prayers for his patient, but at the same time employ all his medical skills to treat him. Two different perspectives may both be valid. A physicist might see a sunset as a refraction of light rays, while a painter might view the same scene as a cascade of colors. Reb Hayim Brisker* observed a sunset on Yom Kippur and described it as the atoning power of the Day of Forgiveness slowly

---

*Rabbi Hayim Soloveichik (1853-1918), one of the predominant Torah leaders of his day, Rav of the Russian town of Brest-Litovsk (Brisk).

sinking below the horizon—an unusual perspective but a perfectly valid one.

Miracles, certainly the miracles of nature, are with us all the time. But, repeating the original question, why don't "supernatural" miracles, the miracles of the second order, happen any more today?

Let us try to answer that question without entering into the various views on the purpose of the Biblical miracles. Take as our case in point the parting of the Red Sea. We are told (Exodus 14:31) that Israel "beheld the hand of G-d" at the Red Sea. The Children of Israel recognized the miracle for what it was. Those generations of the Biblical era to whom it was given to witness miracles had the capability of accepting them as such, and of being impressed.

Then, these ancients implemented their recognition of the "hand of G-d" by living in accordance with the "Word of G-d," because they had experienced Him directly and personally. The generations of antiquity lived in a pre-scientific age. G-d wanted to show them that there was a Power greater than the wealth and the chariots of Pharaoh, greater than the waves of the sea, and they were prepared to learn the lesson which the miracle had been intended to teach.

But people have changed since then. If we were to gather at the banks of the Mississippi River today and I were to promise that, at dawn the next morning, I would strike the river with a staff, and the waters would part, and then, the next morning, I would indeed strike that river a mighty blow and the waters would really part, what would you say? That G-d sent me? That it was a miracle? Or would you suggest that it was a trick which I performed with the aid of a ton of jello under the levee or some other sleight of hand? Or, if we were to meet tomorrow at that mountain in the Sinai desert and to hear a voice thundering forth from a cloud, would we declare that this must be the voice of G-d, or would we suspect the presence of a hidden loudspeaker or some other gadget?

The question we should ask is not whether miracles do or

do not happen today, and why, but what effect miracles would have upon us. Miracles show man that G-d is Master over nature, over all the world. Miracles are a form of communication, but communication needs two partners. To be sure, G-d can perform miracles, but how would *we* react to them? Perhaps, when we are ready for miracles, when we are able to recognize a miracle when we see one, it will be given us to witness miracles.

But then, is it really true that the kind of miracles that are described in the Bible never occur today? I am not a military strategist, but how about the Six-Day War of 1967, and again—more recently and deplorably overlooked— Israel's crossing of the Suez Canal and all the Yom Kippur War? And the Entebbe rescue? I have read many explanations for these events, but frankly, I find it easier to perceive them as miracles which reveal the hand of G-d in the history of man than to accept the "rational" explanations.

The Chosen People

Labels and awareness of identity may be quite innocent, but how can any one people view itself as "chosen"?

The challenge to the concept of a "chosen people" took on serious dimensions particularly within the past generation when the world witnessed the destruction wrought by a people that proclaimed itself the *Herrenvolk*, the master race.

As a result, many Jews today have become timorous about the term "chosen people" as applied to themselves; they have become apologetic for what they now consider the "chauvinism" of their ancestors. Some have even become bitter, for they view "chosen" as having meant—all too often—to be selected for incineration in the ovens of Auschwitz.

Let us begin by clearing the air, so that the term may be analyzed in its own frame of reference, standing or falling on its own merits, and not maligned by considerations that are irrelevant at best, and perverse at worst.

When the Torah speaks of G-d's having "chosen" Israel, the implications are quite clear. The Jews were not chosen to rule over others. They are not heirs to any special privileges. If anything, being "chosen" means that they were selected to bear a special burden of duty and responsibility borne by none other.

Despite our fondness for them, we must realize that democratic ideals and egalitarianism have strictly limited fields of application. Men are definitely not equal, for example, in their natural endowments. Physical vigor is not

uniformly distributed. We may envy an Einstein his intellectual gifts, but they are uniquely his, not ours. We must
take note even of the differences and stratifications artifi-
cially imposed by society. Equal opportunities, equal
franchise, equality before the law are ideals still far from
realization.

Let us look back upon history, as related by the Torah.
Adam, the first man—and any number of his
descendants—had a conception of G-d much as we have it
today; they knew of such ideas as monotheism, morality,
and ethics. The familiar "Seven Commandments of the
Sons of Noah" (described in the essay "Labels") brought
G-d and man together.

However, these religious insights were transmitted only
sporadically, indifferently, and imperfectly. A saintly individual here and there was the exception rather than the
rule. Certainly no perceptible continuity or tradition is
evident until Abraham. Abraham made an effort to share
insights, he had an eagerness to proclaim, teach and dis-
seminate religion. Abraham was not startlingly successful,
for only one of his sons adhered to his teachings.

Abraham was not content with the seven bridges of intermittent communication supplied by the "Seven Commandments." He wanted to *live* in G-d's presence, not only
from time to time, but constantly, not only in certain
sanctified rituals, but in everything that he did and experienced. One generation passed, and then another. Great
numbers could not be persuaded. It seems that outside the
tight little family circle of Abraham and his descendants,
the world remained stonily unmoved. But G-d, the object
of Abraham's worship, was not content that mankind
blunder on interminably. He was not content with the rare
saint. He wanted mankind to know Him, and He chose an
instrument to bear His Word. The descendants of Abraham, that doughty individualist, were to be the worthy
sons of their progenitor. A family—no, a nation—would
now teach mankind about a Being higher than anything
men had known in their world. And that nation was to

teach primarily by living as a testimony to G-d's interest in man, by ordering their lives in accordance with His will.

For this was Israel chosen.

The "choosing" was—we may suggest—mutual. G-d chose Israel, but Israel, and certainly Abraham, also chose G-d. And it may be said that Israel does perform its task. No, not every Jew is a living example of G-d's ideal man; perhaps only few such paragons exist. Nor do all the Jews willingly take up their duty. However, they cannot evade it. For wherever the Jew has wandered, whatever his condition, his identity has persisted and he is identified with those unsettling ideas which his ancestor taught back in ancient Canaan. It is not his personal dedication to Judaism (though that would be much better!) but his very existence that instantly recalls his peculiar status in this world.

There are nations of philosophers, nations of shopkeepers, and so on. But there is only one nation that is the symbol of G-d's concern with man, and that is the Jewish people. We may protest, we may reject our mission, but we are not even permitted the luxury of melting away. Not that Jews have never attempted to do this, or that enemies did not try their worst to erase the symbol. Torquemada and Hitler used physical means that came terrifyingly close to achieving their purpose, and these were only two of many. After over half a century of determination to wipe out Judaism, the powers in Communist Russia are still frantically seeking to erase every vestige of Jewish tradition, and no methods are beneath their dignity. Here we see a world power of the first rank, possessing thermonuclear stockpiles, with vast international influence and apparently global ambitions, resolved to stop a handful of Jews from eating *Matzah* on Passover and taking off a few minutes each day to *daven mincha*.

Is it far-fetched to suggest that the Jewish people represent the antithesis of Hitler, Stalin, and Torquemada? . . .that these tyrants felt such implacable hatred for the Jews because they understood that so long as even one Jew survived, their ideals could never prevail?

This, we suggest, indicates to us the true nature of the mission entrusted to the Jewish people, the purpose for which they were chosen. Would anyone consider this mission too trivial to accept and hold high?

Labels

Students frequently observe that they keep hearing from Chassidim and other Torah Jews about fulfilling ourselves as Jews. Why should we have a particular label? Why can't we simply find personal fulfillment as human beings? There is quite enough challenge in this world facing us as members of the human race without having to assume any particular identity. Would it not be better to erase these artificial barriers that set men apart from one another?

Universalism has a great appeal, and rightfully so; indeed, it is stressed in the Torah that there are religious ideals shared by all mankind. These ideals though deceptively simple, are formidable. The "Seven Commandments of the Sons of Noah," the moral commandments which all men must observe, include the prohibitions against murder, adultery, idolatry, robbery, blasphemy and cruelty to animals. Also, all men are required to devise a code of laws by which to regulate their lives. Note that the "Seven Commandments" serve the needs of society, family, and of the individual as well. But shall we be content with the universal? Must we look down on the particular?

The term "particularism" has acquired an evil connotation because evil men have perverted such concepts as nationality, race and religion to justify some of the worst horrors ever perpetrated by human beings. But this does not mean that it is wrong to consider oneself part of a given nation or religious group. It is neither desirable, or even possible, to escape one's identity.

To have a sense of identity with a particular land, people or faith does not mean that one must therefore feel superior to all others who do not share that identity. Pride in one's own cultural heritage or national history does not imply the right to abuse any human being. Particularism simply implies a matter-of-fact acceptance of the differences that exist between men. We may exchange one identity for another, but we must have some particular identity. We may change over from English to French, but we cannot exist without using some language. Incidentally, countries whose people speak the same language have gone to war against each other. Apparently, then, even the obliteration of separate identities provides no assurance of peace. Nor, in fact, need differences be causes for conflict.

The problem is not the differences that are natural among men, but the arrogance that makes one group consider itself superior to others by virtue of these differences. If we are prepared to accept others as they are without considering them inferior—or ourselves superior—we will have no need to apologize to anyone for the characteristics that are uniquely our own.

When a particular culture is developed, it serves to enrich all mankind. The Flemish painting, the Russian novel, the Italian opera are peculiar to specific countries and nations. They do not come from some vague universalism, but all mankind is welcome to reap whatever benefits it can from these individual creations. It is by being itself that a culture can make its contribution to the whole.

Would it be absurd, then, to suggest that the Torah's insistence on the Jews' preserving their unique identity actually gives Judaism the opportunity to make its contribution to all mankind? The universal ideals expressed in the Torah have laid the groundwork, but they do not necessarily represent the summit.

We would not be doing anyone a favor by foregoing our Jewishness, any more than Beethoven, Rembrandt or Einstein would have served the universal ideal by denying or suppressing their unique talents. Had they done so, they would have deprived mankind of priceless gifts. If we gave up our identity, we, too, would be sinning against our fellow men.

An Accident of Birth

(A response to a student's challenge at an Encounter)

It would appear that being Jewish is a matter of sheer chance, an accident of having been born to Jewish parents. But have we really no choice in this matter?

Here, again, we are dealing with concepts which we accept unquestioningly in their Christian interpretation, without stopping to think whether they are valid in Judaism also. What may be "authentic" for non-Jews is not necessarily applicable to Jews. Is religious affiliation a matter of personal decision? In the "American"—meaning the Christian—conception, it is.

It is a commonplace that the Hebrew language has no true equivalent for the word "religion." American Jews tend to describe Judaism as a "way of life," though how the American Jew's way of life differs from his Gentile neighbor's is not immediately clear. In any case, when we confront Judaism and Jewishness we are not dealing with a mere "religion."

Gentiles "become" Christians at some point in their lives by making a personal decision. They are free at any time to reverse that decision and to cease being Christians. The American Jew tends to apply this mentality to his Judaism and protests that the Torah is seeking to restrict his freedom of choice.

At the outset, let us understand that making choices is not an inalienable right. We are born to a given set of parents without our having had a choice in the matter, even if we warmly approve of our fathers and mothers. The laws of genetics do have something to say about the course of our lives, whether we like it or not. There's little we can do to change this. Frustrating, perhaps, but there it is.

Of course we have innumerable choices in other areas, especially in an open democratic society. We are reasonably free to choose our friends, our occupations, and our political affiliations.

Into which category does Judaism fit? Are we Jews by "the law of genetics" or are we free to choose whether we want to be Jews? The Gentile apparently regards his religious identity as a matter of his own choice, to be accepted, rejected, or changed at will. But why should we Jews force our thinking into non-Jewish molds? Let us explore the Jewish view on this subject.

Note: there is no such thing as a "Christian atheist." The two terms "Christian" and "atheist" are mutually exclusive. But there are Jews who assert that they are atheists and yet furiously insist that they are Jews. Of course they will define "Jewishness" in nationalistic terms, Jews by nationality, say, just as other Jews who will just as vigorously deny that they are anything else but Americans, Frenchmen, or Englishmen.

We have been dealing until now with elements external to the person—his beliefs, his society, his way of thinking and living. These are not the person himself. But when the Torah speaks of the Jew it refers to his essence, his very being, his "I." This is what the Jew *is*, and it is not subject to whim or change. My selfhood is not a suit of clothes to be discarded as styles change, neither is my Jewishness. My "I" is constant; my Jewishness, too, is forever unchanging.

We may accept our parents or reject them but they remain our parents nonetheless. We can fulfill our obligations toward them or neglect them, but the obligations remain. We can accept our Jewishness joyously and gratefully, or we can attempt to escape it. But whatever we do does not change the situation. We are still Jews.

Chassidus has some insights to offer in the assumptions of the original question—that of the fortuitous circumstance of birth. The Baal Shem Tov emphasized *hashgacha p'ratis,* the concept of individual Divine Providence. An accident is without purpose or sense. But, as the Baal Shem Tov teaches, there really are no "accidents" in our lives. Every experience, every occurrence has meaning and purpose. We are not actors in some theater of the absurd. What is the meaning, the purpose, the sense of things? We do not always know, but of this we are sure: there is purpose in our being born Jewish, not the blind workings of an impersonal fate, an "accident of birth." The options before us are to deny purpose, to attempt to escape from ourselves, to suppress the essence-spark within us—or to affirm what we are, to make our Jewishness an opportunity for growth, to fulfill our purpose in being.

Nothing human is trivial or "accidental," certainly not the momentous event of birth.

Anti-Semitism
and Jewish Survival
(A reply to a student's question at an Encounter)

Is the survival of Judaism dependent on anti-Semitism? Wasn't persecution always a major force in the preservation of the Jewish people? It seems that whenever Jews have liberty, they soon cast off their Jewish identity and assimilate into the society in which they live. It is often pointed out that the great Jewish religious and cultural treasures of the past are products of the ghetto, in which Jews were barred from the universities and professions, but that once the ghetto walls had fallen, the Jews became such eager participants in the culture of the non-Jewish world that in the process their own Jewish heritage was lost.

But should all this really lead us to believe that we are confronted with the dismal alternatives of either persecution and spiritual growth or freedom and spiritual decline?

It is important to remember that until Hitler every Jew was free to escape persecution if he so desired. If he accepted the cross (or the crescent), his life and safety were assured and his economic position vastly improved. We see then that it was not persecution that kept the Jew close to his Jewishness. The stick of persecution was always accompanied by the carrot of conversion. But except for a few, the Jews always rejected the carrot with contempt. Only with Hitler was the Jew denied the choice.

However, you pointed out, and with considerable justification, that Jews did assimilate in frightening numbers under liberal Western regimes such as pre-Hitler Germany. The American experience is hardly reassuring. Let us turn to a brief phrase the Alter Rebbe used in his *Tanya*, the fundamental work of *Chabad Chassidus.*

In discussing the "spirit of foolishness" that leads man to sin, the founder of Chabad explains that the "foolishness" consists of man's delusion that *odenu b'yahaduso,* his "Jewishness" is unimpaired by what he does. When a "fool" is tempted to sin, he will rationalize and persuade himself that even if he sins he is still a "good Jew." But, as R. Schneur Zalman goes on to explain, this is not true. With every sin he commits, the individual severs part of the link between himself and G-d until the bond has been completely sundered.

The first Lubavitcher Rebbe then proceeds to point out that whenever the Jew confronts a moral decision without delusions, whenever he must make a clear-cut choice between apostasy and martyrdom, he will be ready to give his life rather than to forsake his Judaism. It is obvious to him that once he has converted, he will no longer be a Jew, and this choice is unacceptable to him.

It is only in the less dramatic decisions, which he does not perceive as threats to his Jewishness, that the individual will permit the "spirit of foolishness" to assert itself. "Well, then, I'll miss this *mitzvah,* or forget about that *mitzvah,*" he tells himself, "but I'll still be a Jew."

In the lands of persecution, conversion held no charms for the Jew because he immediately realized what conversion would mean. And so he clung tenaciously to his Jewishness because the alternative was out of the question. He proudly asserted his Jewishness, lived it deeply and richly, and outlived his tormentors.

In the lands of assimilation, on the other hand, the choice never appears to be quite so clear-cut. The erosion of Jewish values is a gradual one; the inroads of assimilation are so subtle as to be almost imperceptible at any given moment. The process might take a generation and longer, and often it is only when his son or daughter brings home the Gentile he or she intends to marry that the drifting Jew realizes what he has allowed to happen to his Judaism. But by that time it is already quite late.

In recapitulation; yes, it is true that Judaism seemed to persevere more in lands of religious persecution, where the only other alternative open to the Jew was outright conversion, than in countries where freedom tempted the Jew to assimilate without having to decide on the spot whether or not he was ready to give up his religion for the dominant faith. Yes, Judaism flourished in the Russia of Tsarist tyranny and eroded in the France of "liberty, equality, fraternity." But this does not mean that tyranny is a healthy climate for the Jew—or for Judaism. Oppression is not conducive to great literature or religion. Oppression brutalizes. The occasional saint may be refined by suffering, but for the bulk of more ordinary humanity, oppression is thoroughly unrewarding, no matter how one looks at it. Negative forces don't yield positive results. The flowering of Jewish life centuries ago in Central Europe, and more recently in Poland and Lithuania was generated not by pressures from without, but by energies from within.

The breakdown of the ghetto walls, the conferment of civil rights upon all citizens, regardless of religion—these developments in themselves need not pose a threat to Jewish survival. They are, however, very much a challenge to Jews and to Judaism. In periods of pre-Auschwitz persecution, the Jew was much more aware of the ultimate consequences of his every defection from Torah than he generally is in countries where no one holds out to him the bait of conversion as the price of his freedom. But the remedy for this lack of awareness in the midst of liberty is not a return to the ghetto; instead, it should be an increased sensitivity to the fact that no act, no moral decision of ours, is so insignificant that it will not affect our own Jewish survival, and that of our children.

Chassidic Attitudes
to Other Jews
(Address to a group of Jewish social workers)

The Jewish attitude toward other Jews is not monolithic. Of course we know that all Jews are responsible for one another, but I want to go beyond this, in hopes of being able to bring you some new insights. Perhaps the title of my presentation should really be "The Jewish Attitude Toward Other *Kinds* of Jews," toward Jews with whom we disagree, perhaps violently.

We can describe two basic orientations within the Torah community. I use the term "Torah community" for two reasons. First, because this is the area with which I am most familiar. Secondly, these two orientations are drawn from their Torah background, with a minimum of influence from the non-Torah world.

1. "Enclave Judaism" and "Activist Judaism"

One camp in the Torah community consists of the inward-looking, modern *"shtetl-type"* community. The other is represented by *Chabad*-Lubavitch and others who share their view on the relations between observant and non-observant Jews. We might call the first community the *enclave* and the second, the *activist*.

The enclave community is inward-directed, concerned only with its own perpetuation, with preserving and developing itself, with transmitting Torah and *Yiddishkeit* to their own children and their own adherents. They have achieved remarkable levels of Torah scholarship and *mitzvah* observance, and have been enviably successful in perpetuating their communities. In these circles assimilation is virtually unknown. On the other hand, their influence, at least their direct impact on the rest of the Jewish world, is small. They are fearful lest involvement with the non-committed may somehow dilute the commitment of their own people, that instead of influencing the non-observant to keep *mitzvot,* they themselves might become weaker in their own convictions and observances. These communities are oases, lush and verdant, in a barren wilderness, a desert bare of vegetation, a world that shows little promise for the future. The overwhelming majority of America's 6,000,000 Jews stand in sorry contrast to the *elan,* the scholarship, and dedication of the relatively few thousands in America's enclave communities. The enclave community considers the outlook for the outsiders to be little short of hopeless, and feels that it has enough to do within its own ranks, preserving and deepening its own roots.

Not so the activists, particularly *Chabad*-Lubavitch. *Chabad*-Lubavitch stresses an ancient Torah concept, namely, that all Jews are responsible for one another, in more than the material sense. No Jew is an island of virtue surrounded by a sea of Jewish indifference. The founder of *Chabad* went so far as to say that a Jew who helps another Jew to regain his Jewishness will find his own heart and mind purified and refined "a thousandfold." One's own development and improvement are not achieved by concentrating on one's own growth, but by giving attention to those around him as well. In helping others the Jew helps himself also.

2. Some Chassidic Doctrines

I shall try to present this paper from the *Chassidic* perspective, with no pretensions of being "universal" and with no expectations of avoiding controversy. It is a small matter to devise lofty moral declarations, but it is quite another thing to base them upon a firm underpinning, where the morality is a product of an *Anschauung* rather than a statement in a vacuum. The Lubavitcher attitudes stem ineluctably from fundamental *Chabad* concepts about G-d and man; they are part of a consistent whole, a system rather than a sentiment.

At the outset let me make this general statement about the views of the Lubavitch movement: we recognize no valid distinctions separating one Jew from another. There are no Orthodox Jews, or Conservative, or Reform, or secular, or what-have-you Jews. There are only *Jews,* period. Or exclamation point! We are all part of an unbroken continuum; some of us are more learned, more observant than others, but Moses and we are links in the same chain. Before any misinterpretations arise, let me stress that I am speaking here of Jews as individuals, not of "movements" or "branches" or "variations" on Judaism. There is one valid Judaism and a less genuine Judaism (there's a value judgment for you, and a delicate euphemism), but there is no such thing as a fractional Jew. Let's study some *Chassidus* together and see what happens.

Chassidus, or chassidic doctrines, explains the difference between *etzem,* ("essence") and *hispashtus,* ("extension"). Man thinks, he has emotions, he speaks and acts. The relations we establish with others are generally governed by these manifestations of man—his words, his ideas, his values, his actions, and so on. We might be attracted by them or repelled; we may admire them or detest them. We will accept or reject the others on this basis. *Chassidus* describes these manifestations as outward, external expressions of the soul, of the person, but they are not the person himself. Man is not identical with his actions, his words, his thoughts, his values, or his strengths or weaknesses. These manifestations are, or should be, in a state of constant growth, flux, development, they should be dynamic, never stagnant. These are the "possessions," the "extensions" of the person, but they are not the person as such. Man *has* these ideas, feelings and so forth. But what *is* he? What is his irreducible essence, his constant core, his ultimate self? *Chassidus* proposes s simple answer: his essence is his *soul.* "Soul" is a vague term which *Chassidus* defines as a spark of G-d, no less. Hence, when we reject any Jew, we reject a spark of G-d, and though we are doubtless highly virtuous and saintly, this is a thing we are not quite qualified to do.

This sort of approach helps make familiar but difficult passages and doctrines in the Torah intelligible and logical. For example: on the face of it, the commandment, "Love your fellow like yourself" is a fine sentiment but wholly unrealistic. It is precisely the sort of thing the skeptic would expect to hear from the pulpit; pious platitudes unrelated to the human condition. How can *I* love *you* like myself? I am I; you are you. My stubbed toe is infinitely more distressing to me than the horrors of Biafra and Bangladesh. When I miss breakfast the sky starts to fall in at about 10 A.M., but the real anguish of another person doesn't disturb the even tenor of our lives. For the materialist, the barriers that separate men from one another are insuperable obstacles. By "materialist" I mean one whose orientation is toward the physical world, who defines man in "body" terms, who recognizes only what he can see and evaluate; in brief, one whose universe is circumscribed by the inherent inescapable limitations of the observable, measurable and quantitative. Once we accept G-d, and the fact that He has placed a spark of Himself within each of us, the barriers separating men from one another disappear. My "I" and your "you" are distinct only when "I" and "you" are defined in material terms ("material" includes esthetic, emotional, intellectual, as well as bodily).

However, when man is not seen as a body, and humanity is defined not in terms of physical posture or ability to use tools, or even verbal communication, but as a personified spark of G-d, that man does not merely react to stimuli but is capable of making moral decisions, who is something more than a product of environment and influences, then mankind becomes a community. We are more than individual bodies; we are sparks from one Source, not different, not separate. "Love your fellow like yourself" is not a pious platitude but a realistic challenge, bidding you to recognize that your fellowman is not "another," but a part of your very self, that when you reject him you reject part of your own self, and that, conversely, when you help him you come closer to your own fulfillment, for he and you are not unrelated entities.

Nowhere here is there any implication that you must accept the particular conduct of another without qualifications. Man's task as a human being is that he make his externals, the "extension" of his soul, his words and deeds and emotions and thoughts consonant with the internal, the essence of man, the G-d-spark within him. Dissonance within the individual, inward discord, conflict between the inalienable surge of the soul and the crass indulgences of the body or ego, are to be eliminated or, as *Chassidus* realistically teaches, reduced, so that the soul can dominate, and the fulfillment of the soul becomes man's goal in life. This approach of *Chabad Chassidus,* differentiating between the essence of man and his outwardness, addressing one's self to the essence, appealing to its "Jewishness" and attempting to disentangle it from its encumbrances of habit and extraneous influences, probably explains part of the remarkable success Chassidim have had in communicating with hippies, alienated students, left-wing kibbutzniks, and Jews in the Soviet Union.

Another aspect of this approach is the avoidance, as much as humanly possible, of condescension, of a holier-than-thou attitude, of preachment. Over two centuries ago the founder of *Chabad* taught that the sheltered Bet Hamedrash Jew, the scholarly and pious privileged to devote himself to Torah study without distraction, ought not feel superior to the less learned market-place Jew. The latter constantly faces distraction and temptation. Too, he may by nature be more passionate. His comparatively modest achievements in Torah and piety are qualitatively more valued, for "the reward is in accordance with the burden."

Now back to that word "materialism." *Mitzvot,* virtues, cannot be compared and totted up. In the same manner, one individual cannot be compared to another. The Torah tells us that Moses was the most humble of men. He knew that objectively he was superior to his contemporaries, he must have been aware of his learning, his saintliness, his gift of prophecy. What, then, did his humility mean? His humility lay in that he saw his virtues not as products of his own efforts, but as gifts from G-d. He knew that ordinary individuals had to struggle for each achievement of the spirit, no matter how insignificant, for every victory over temptation, and Moses felt that G-d treasured such hard-won accomplishments of mind and spirit far more than those which he, Moses, had attained without that effort on his part.

Perhaps this sounds a little idealistic, but it is a fact nonetheless: the recognition that the one who is taught by the *Chassid* is doing more for the *Chassid* than the *Chassid* is doing for him, that his faltering attempts at *davening,* at keeping a moment of Shabbos, at putting on *tefillin,* are more valued than the piety of the *Chassid.* Please note that this is not some mawkish sentimentality, but a value system, a perspective on man and world and G-d. It's easy to say that the simple illiterate is better than the scholar, but the *Chassid* makes every effort to find a concrete justification for regarding the other man as his own superior. He is not engaged in parlor spirituality but in rough and demanding human relations, with himself as one of the partners in these relationships.

In summation, according to the Chassidic view, the relationship of the Jew with other Jews might be summed up as follows:

1. Distinctions among Jews are artificial, superficial, misleading and false.
2. We must never reject a fellow Jew, even if we do not approve of everything he does.

3. Condescension toward the recipient of a favor, be that favor spiritual or material, is an unacceptable distortion of the proper relationship.

Historically the elimination of the barriers between the scholarly class and the ignorant was one of the early revolutions brought about by *Chassidus*. In a sense, the generally prevalent view in the early 18th century, when *Chassidus* first came upon the scene, was that the love of one's fellow men had to be earned by personal virtue, and the supreme personal virtue was Talmudic scholarship. The Baal Shem Tov, founder of *Chassidus* asserted that the relationship between G-d and Israel is that of parent and child, and no child is any *more* the child of his parents than any of the others. "You cannot despise the child and still love the Father," a Chassidic aphorism goes. "You shall love the L-rd your G-d" and "You shall love your fellow man" are parallels, one rebbe noted. Which of these two precepts comes first? The observance of the precept to "love your fellow man," we are told, is the first step toward fulfilling the precept to "love your G-d." A father should be aware of his child's faults, but he will not humiliate him or reject him on that account.

There is a rather enigmatic law in the Torah that prohibits the direct counting of Jews at any gathering. Even when we count the number of men in *Shul* to see whether the mandatory quorum (*Minyan*) of ten is present, we do not count, "One, two, three . . . " etc. but use other devices such as a Biblical verse of ten words, or the Yiddish euphemism, "*Not* one, *not* two," with the smug explanation that "I'm NOT counting." It sounds trivial, perhaps, but it has unsuspected values to declare.

When we count, the units being counted must be similar and the more units the greater the sum. We count things that are alike. But we cannot count people, because every human being is unique, *sui generis,* unduplicated. We may not be aware that a certain individual we know is unique; he seems to be most unspectacular and even expendable. Maybe this is what G-d meant when He told Abraham that his seed would be like the stars of heaven—seemingly tiny, but only because we are so far away from them. Get closer to the other man and you will see greatness—perhaps even enough to dwarf you.

A *Chassid* who happened to be a diamond dealer once asked a Lubavitcher Rebbe why he made such a fuss over simple Jews. "What is so great about them?" The Rebbe's explanations did not convince the questioner. A little later the Rebbe asked the man to show him some of the stones he was selling and to explain their value. After the jeweler had shown the Rebbe the different stones, the Rebbe said, "I don't see any difference between one diamond and the other." The *Chassid* answered, "Rebbe, you have to a *maivin* (expert) to see the difference." "Oh," the Rebbe answered him, "if you have to be a *maivin* to appreciate a stone, how much more of a *maivin* must you be to appreciate a human soul!" So whether it's a rabbi dealing with a congregant, a physician with a patient, or a social worker with a client, a bit of humility and respect is quite in order.

Human beings are qualities, not quantities. A number defines, sets limits; that is *it,* no more, no less. Two is twice as much as one, a million is a million times one. But in dealing with human beings, statistical methods are out of place and misleading unless used with great caution. People are not statistics; they are qualities. Two symphonies are not twice as much as one symphony. Man is made in the image of G-d; he is therefore an infinity. Two infinities—if you will ignore the contradiction in terms there—are not twice as much as one infinity. This is not just an exercise in wordgames, intellectual acrobatics; life-and-death laws hinge on it. You don't sacrifice one life for many, because many lives are not worth more than one life. No matter how noble your motivation, you do not shorten any life by even one moment, because one moment is no less in quality than the Biblical life span of 70 years. The implications for those privileged to follow careers helping people are clear. This attitude, I suggest, is the most humanizing view of man I have ever encountered, and the consequences of this view keep us from depersonalizing ourselves and others.

3. Notes on Values and Objectivity

The ideal of objectivity is a chimera. It might be applicable to certain sciences, but it has little application in most human affairs. We are constantly making value judgments and should not need to apologize for it. There is a fundamental obstacle to so-called objectivity: objectivity itself is a value judgment, for it implies that the subjects under discussion are equal to one another. This, I submit, is as much a commitment as any declaration in favor of one subject over the other. Hence the veneer of objectivity is misleading; an admitted bias would at least be more honest. I might be able to discuss the relative merits of say, Shintoism and Zen, and do it objectively, but it will be clear that my very objectivity indicates that I do have an attitude toward them, namely indifference. I suggest that we remember that when we deal directly with other human beings. A university seminar may be able to afford the luxury of exploration without restraint (and I do believe the university ought to understand that it is responsible for the consequences of its own unexpressed biases), but when we deal with people who, often under stress and deeply concerned with the matter under discussion, can be affected by the spoken and the unsaid, by nuances and facial expressions, we must be exceedingly aware and careful of what we do. Whether we like it or not, we exercise an influence over our clients, and we must consider not only how we feel in fact, but what the client thinks we feel.

I suspect that defining values in today's Jewish world is frequently a matter of accepting certain stances as normative and even "Jewish." There is a feeling that values described as "liberal" in our society are identical with Jewish values. For example, there is the current acceptance of abortion, in which many Jews join without even thinking to ask whether Judaism actually agrees with this view. The usual rationale is: a woman owns her body, therefore she has the right to decide what to do with it. If she wished to terminate a pregnancy, it is her concern, and hers alone. The inference is that any impingement on this right is *prima facie* unacceptable and must be justified before it can be countenanced. The "normative" or objective attitude would be to accept abortion; the "value judgment" would be to qualify such acceptance. I am not at the moment concerned with the substantive question of abortion, but with the definition of objectivity and commitment. We have presumptions, unconscious perhaps, but real just the same.

One of the reasons I believe the *Chassidim* have been able to penetrate circles that seemed impervious to Judaism is that *Chassidim* are non-judgmental. However, I must emphasize that I use the term "non-judgmental" in a special way. "Non-judgmental" is not the same as "indifferent," non-evaluating, or approving. A university dean justified the elimination of grades at his institution by explaining that we live in a non-judgmental society. This is not what I mean. *Chassidim* do have standards, values, concepts of right and wrong. However, they are non-condemning, non-rejecting; they accept the *individual,* whatever he might be. A "non-judgmental" attitude may degenerate into a stance of flaccidity, everything-is-as-good-as-everything-else, loss of standards, elimination of excellence, shoddiness, be it in intellect, morals, art or workmanship. This is an evasion of responsibility and will be tolerated only in certain areas until there is a popular revolt. For example, professors at medical schools had better be judgmental right now!

In terms of family and children's services and related fields, I suggest that placing all alternatives and views on a par is neither "scientific" nor "objective." Perhaps the very adjective "Jewish" in the name of your agency indicates a commitment. To me, at least, the adjective implies that the objectives of your agency are not always consonant with what happens to be popular and acceptable in America at the moment. Being *au courant* is not the highest conceivable accolade; running with any pack is not a mark of independence. Judaism, however you wish to define it, has certain values with which social workers must be familiar, no matter how you choose to present them to your clients. Besides abortion, which we have already mentioned, there are such problems as adoption, divorce, care of the aged, family responsibilities (another *gauche* word today), birth control, and so on. The point is that unfortunately, there is no "neutral" ground. Any position you take, including supposed "indifference," is in fact, an involvement.

The agency's concern about its responsibilities toward the community is a valid one. But the way in which a *Jewish* agency fulfills that responsibility is by giving paramount consideration to the *Jewish* attitude toward the problems with which it is called upon to cope. By "the Jewish attitude" I mean the attitude of Judaism as set forth in the sources hallowed by Jewish tradition. There are areas of potential, even inevitable disagreement, and these will have to be given due consideration. But beyond these, there are immense areas where the Jewish view is clear, and if one takes issue with that view one does so from a premise other than Judaism. We must assert our independence from the fads and fashions of the moment, and retain our own values. We need not be in the forefront of every transitory movement that the media propagate as being "in" at the moment.

Since you represent a family agency it is appropriate to address ourselves to the family, especially the Jewish view of what the family is. The unfortunate family has fallen upon hard times. Time was when G-d, Flag and Mother were sacrosanct. G-d can still take care of Himself, and there is a huge bureaucracy to defend the Flag. But Mother, and the family, are left almost defenseless against serious attacks. The touted obsolescence of the family, alternative life-styles, new family structures, trial marriages, replacements of the traditional family structure by communal institutions, the rising divorce rate, so-called "arrangements," innovations *ad nauseam*—these are all commonplace today. Parenthetically, our Sages tell us that our idol-worshipping ancestors knew paganism was nonsense, but it was a good excuse for licentiousness . . . The economic function of the family has diminished in importance; therefore, the whole institution is being scrapped. The new so-called "moralities," though that specific noun is a bit dated, have no use for traditional family bonds; they serve only as another excuse for rejecting the family.

No matter how much you pay someone for the work he does, it is vital that he feel his work is important. Hire a man to sit for eight hours and look at the wall and he will quit in disgust, not because he is bored but because he feels useless. This, by the way, is the reason why so many gifted young people today are reluctant to enter the field of Jewish education, outside the Day School movement. They feel that the results of their labors don't matter very much. A first-grade teacher in a public school may be starting a Nobel Laureate on his—or her—way. The public school teacher is certainly teaching skills and knowledge indispensable in the world in which the student lives. The "Hebrew teacher," on the other hand, may feel that what he—or she—teaches is an unnecessary luxury, a matter of supreme irrelevance in today's world. Pension plans will not make the field any more attractive; only a sense that it's all worthwhile can do that.

The family situation is a close parallel to this. There is a mindless trend to denigrate the importance of family, and since the central figure in the family is the mother, she is demeaned, explicitly or implicitly, as a "mere" housewife (like the "mere" teacher). If the mother is made to feel that her work is trivial and useless, how can she have pride in herself? How can she overcome the inevitable frustrations and problems of rearing a family? Small wonder that family agencies have clients. I would expect that many unhappy women can't even identify their malaise; they do not even associate their distress with the role assigned to the mother and family by today's society. As a result, they become emotional problems and worse. I don't intend to enter the issue of Women's Liberation at this time but I suggest that undiscriminating enthusiasm, the uncritical mouthing of slogans, can be as destructive and harmful as the attitudes one wishes to correct.

Once a young girl came to see me. She had graduated from a fine Eastern university with honors and came to Music City, as Nashville humbly calls itself. The child was shattered emotionally and physically, but she kept talking about her one "success"—a singing TV commercial for dog food. This is what passes as "creative" in today's world of slogans. Transforming a tiny blob of flesh into a feeling and thinking human being lacks glamor. The girl could not imagine that raising a family could provide challenges and satisfaction.

Speaking from the Jewish or rabbinic perspective, the tragedy of the young people today is not the conventionally "religious" problem of a "lost generation," serious though that is. It is a *human* problem of staggering consequence. Such evils as drugs, gurus, eastern cults, communes, are only symptoms; they reflect the groping of the young for a mother, a father, a family and human warmth. One teen-age guru had Jewish students paying $5 each in cash for the privilege of kissing his foot. This is not a fairy-tale; it really happened.

Alienation is directly related to motherless homes, and this is not only true for small children but also in the case of teen-age youth. These young people are lost, not only to Judaism but also, as the Lubavitcher Rebbe has said, to decency, goodness and holiness. The degree of indifference to another person can be shocking. I know of a father who suddenly lost both of his own parents and, as a result, became severely depressed. But his children could not see why they should even pay him a visit. Witness the converse of this: at a convention of the World Union of Jewish Students, a young girl told us that she had been pleading with her mother to make their home kosher. When her parents moved to another house, she thought it was the best time to ask them again. "Hey, Ma, how about going kosher?" "Do you know what my mother did?" the student asked. "She laughed. That's what she did. She laughed. And know what I did? I cried. I'm still crying."

Rav Hadakov, the Rebbe's secretary, once noted that the home has disintegrated to such a degree that children simply don't understand why there should be special filial feelings, or love among family members. The young are blundering and groping, not even knowing what they seek. They feel lost and alone, because father and mother are too busy, he with making a living, she with social obligations.

The Rebbe spoke at length about the family *as family,* not as a group of people but as a unit. Whether or not the family is truly a family depends in a unique way on the mother. If she does not regard her function as worthy, then any efforts by the rest of the family are doomed to failure. She must bring to her family warmth, closeness and feeling so that all the members of her family will be drawn close together into one cohesive whole. The breakups of family life and the shocking number of precious young lives forfeited are the result of the family's failure to provide the family quality.

Financial independence? What have these to do with human warmth? If ever the family was needed it is today. If ever a human function was priceless, it is the function of creating a family, and—I might suggest—showing and encouraging others how to create true families of their own with the family quality. To be sure, you might then work yourselves out of your jobs—but let's not worry too much about that.

I referred to the popular argument that changes in the economic structure of society, the financial independence of wife and children, make the classical family obsolete. This argument has another basic fallacy. Again, let us cite a Chassidic insight. The Baal Shem Tov commented on the famous Biblical verse, "Not on bread alone does man live" (Deut. 8:3). He said that when bread is "alone," when man can see nothing except bread, he cannot live. When a man sees every aspect of life only in terms of bread, of material benefits, he cannot live as a truly human being. And a man who lives not like a human but like an animal suffers horribly. Though he feels free to cater to all his desires and does not feel bound by obligation, duties, disciplines, or restraints, happiness will elude him. Man cannot have his bread alone; he needs an appropriate framework to live a truly human life.

In the materialist view the physical is the crucial element in life. For him, the whole structure of human relationships, even the bonds between husband and wife, parents and children, is dependent on economics, on financial arrangements. The cottage industries in which families developed bonds of interdependence because they worked side by side to sustain the whole have long been replaced by factories, laboratories and offices which separate the families physically during the working day, and also emotionally after work is done. The family's former economic functions, say the materialists, created the most meaningful and enduring bonds, but now that the family is no longer an economic unit, it is falling apart. Relations between husband and wife, parents and children, are secondary. Man-woman relationships may be formed on a temporary basis, say, for a year, after which both partners are free to go their own ways. Who needs these people any more? Give them "freedom" to choose for themselves.

It is in this area that the eternity and immutability of Torah find critically needed expression. "Honor your father and your mother" is not contingent on an economic system, or on conditions in any given area, or on social approval. To honor one's parents is an eternal *mitzvah*; so, too, is the commandment (addressed to parents) to "teach (the precepts of G-d) diligently to your children." And the family, the framework within which both these commandments are translated into living reality, is eternal.

The family is the core unit of Jewry, its primary institution. It is the first and most important school for our young. It is the means of transmitting a heritage and culture. School—including religious schools, synagogues, indeed all public institutions, are only ancillary to the family. These institutions may wither, but as long as the family flourishes, they will all be revived. However, if they all flourish, but the family is allowed to disintegrate, then I have serious misgivings about the future.

The HOLOCAUST*

The common approach to the questions posed by the
Holocaust is to attempt to explain what kind of G-d could
have permitted an Auschwitz, what is His relationship to
the world of man, and what attitude we should adopt
toward Him. Some who never believed in G-d found their
atheism or agnosticism reinforced—though citing Auschwitz as justification for every cheap self-indulgence is
unspeakably vile. Others, formerly believers, may have rejected their faith. On the other hand, a remarkable number
of Holocaust survivors emerged with a faith and devotion
we can only admire and humbly envy.

Still, the question continues to haunt us, and the answers
still elude us. We will never be able to justify the Holocaust,
to rationalize it, to explain why it occurred. It is simply
impossible for any of us even to attempt such a thing. The
Holocaust is beyond our comprehension, and we cannot
explain matters that exceed our understanding. We who
were not in concentration camps cannot possibly conceive
what it was like, and those who were interned in Dachau or
Buchenwald before the outbreak of World War II cannot
picture Treblinka.

But while we cannot understand the Holocaust, we dare
not fail to learn from it what we can. If it is beyond our
power to discern the workings of Providence in the cre-
matoria, we may still learn something of the nature and

---

*This essay may be regarded as an extension of "Uses of Torah."

workings of man, and perhaps draw some warranted conclusions.

There was a time when man had rather romantic dreams of human perfectibility, of a generally upward trend in history, of man evolving above savagery and barbarism. Civilization and culture, education and scholarship, science and the arts—all the achievements of mankind, it was believed, raised man above the level of the beast. The cannibals, the "mountains of skulls," were the stuff of the primitives, inconceivable in the new world of progress. To be sure, the line of man's rise was not consistently upward; there were moments of retrogression, of backsliding, but the trend of history seemed to be unmistakably upward. Barbarism was a thing of the past.

The carnage of World War I dulled the sheen of idealism somewhat; Utopia was not so close at hand, after all. But certain basic concepts of man and culture persisted. With Darwinism (which is often misapplied by uncritical enthusiasts—whatever its merits in biology, it is not necessarily relevant to literature, religion, history and morality) and the development of such studies as archeology, Biblical criticism, and anthropology, the influence of religion was weakened and in many instances destroyed altogether. Certainties and absolute standards were dismissed. Studies of comparative culture taught that what might be considered wrong in one society might be regarded as quite appropriate behavior in another. Family structures varied and economic arrangements differed from culture to culture. Right and wrong were no longer considered absolutes; morality had become a relative concept.

The inference was obvious: it was man who determined morality, and man's circumstances and opinions may vary. Seen from this vantage point, an old morality may become obsolete in the face of a new context which will give rise to a "new" morality. And since context is the determinant, it is assumed that the new is always "better" in its world than the old would be. Conceived in broad terms, this doctrine was not particularly unsettling, for it seemed certain that there was in man's nature some innate quality—let us call it humanism—that would insure the preservation of universal ideals. One society may be matriarchal, another patriarchal, and a third may be a monarchy, each strikingly different from the others, of course, but these differences were considered trivial in the face of the humanity they supposedly all held in common. The "core morality" would endure. Thus, reverence for life was cited as an example of universal human morality, not subject to fluctuation and rejection in the civilized world. But as for the finer points of the traditional morality, the Biblical ethos, they were cavalierly dismissed as trivia.

Let us digress for a moment. The classical philosophers struggled to define good and evil without particular success, certainly without achieving a consensus. The scientist refuses to make value judgments; he will not admit terms such as "right" and "wrong" into his professional vocabulary, and quite properly so, for he deals only with quantities, with things that can be observed and verified. His conclusions will be accepted without reference to nationality or religion, or to any prior commitment or prejudice. But the tools of the scientist are not equipped to deal with variables, with subjective concepts such as morality. The philosopher's "tool," his intellect, also cannot cope with right and wrong, for cold logic does not prefer one interpretation over another. Intellectually, polygamy is neither superior nor inferior to monogamy, and "marital arrangements" are neither "right" nor "wrong." One arrangement apparently works for some people while others prefer some other system. Nothing has been proven about innate "rightness" or "goodness." Every moral judgment is subject to the same fate—philosophy cannot logically declare one or the other to be right.

The atmosphere in the philosopher's seminar is rarefied and not always directly involved in worldly affairs. Men of affairs may know little and care even less about the philosopher's quandaries.

But, it was argued, even if the close argumentation and

rigorous logic of scholars preclude any statement from that quarter on good and evil, man still had recourse to his "instinct," his human-ness. He *knew* that killing was wrong. The philosopher knew that even if he would be unable to produce a definition of evil, man would still live by principle. People would continue to be "moral."

Unhappily, however, some people adopted the arguments of the anthropologists and philosophers and took them seriously. Society would determine what was right and what was wrong, and do it with a vengeance. Once the majority culture decided that an entire people was inferior, it became "right" to destroy that people, and Auschwitz was spawned. The society of Hitler's Germany enthusiastically endorsed the "new morality." But if it is "society" that decides what is right, which society is it to be, mine, yours, or the Nazi's? The Nazis simply made a logical application of situation ethics. Why, then, the furor over Auschwitz? The moral relativists have long rejected G-d and His strictures. They think in human terms. Why are they so upset about the Holocaust? If one accepts the thesis that any "society" is the sole arbiter of right and wrong for its members, at what point does one consider that the German society lost its credentials as a full-fledged society fit to make its own policies?

At the beginning of the 1930's the moral relativists still stood on firm ground. Who would have imagined then that in the 20th century, in the heart of "civilized" Europe, a nation of scientists and philosophers would become a nation of SS guards capable of murdering one million children? Even now, over three decades after the fact and with so much literature readily available on the subject, there are too many who still cannot quite believe that Auschwitz ever really existed. The logical conclusions of moral relativism may have been inevitable in a discussion, but that generation, in its blithe naiveté, saw them as nothing more than an impossible nightmare. No matter what its origin, the dictum "thou shalt not kill" would be an eternal declaration of human sentiment. Today, however, we know that man is indeed capable of pursuing the logic of moral relativism to its most horrifying conclusion. The alternative to an "objective" morality is not relativism ("this" or "that" morality) but rather "no-morality" or "a-morality." What is more, we cannot expect this new amorality to respect any sancta, to preserve any values that are cherished today. The question is not *where* to draw the line—though the implications of this alone are grave enough—but whether *any* line at all may be drawn at any point.

The supposed "civilizing" effects of culture, learning and intellectuality have been placed in grave doubt. There is no obvious correlation between intellectual superiority and moral excellence. One's mind may improve through study, but the effects of study on character and morality may be something less than profound and decisive. Though their preeminence in their respective specialties was beyond dispute, the professors of Nazi Germany certainly did not cover themselves with glory when it came to moral accomplishments.

Let us move closer to home. Suppose we give each society the authority to evolve its own definition of right and wrong. Why, then, could not a Ku Klux Klan society be permitted to define right and wrong in its own way? You happen to disagree with the Nazi or KKK definitions of morality? Then formulate your own definitions, but do not denounce the Nazis or the Ku Klux Klan as evil, or as monsters, and do not wrap yourself in the mantle of righteousness. Do you want to fight them? Again, the final decision will be one of force and if the Ku Kluxers, or the Nazis, happen to be stronger than you, well, then . . . There is still considerable sentiment in Germany that Hitler's sole crime was to have lost World War II.

But back to our original problem, the Holocaust. Here we have one lesson we can learn from Auschwitz: the Holocaust has taught us what man *can* be. When man alone is permitted to decide how to live his life, the product may be either a saint or a demon, but the one will be as justifiable and legitimate as the other. If man is to live by the kind of moral standard which will make it impossible for another Auschwitz to occur, it must be an objective standard, imposed from outside of man, or else it will twist to accommodate itself to whatever man wants. The Jew who has the Torah as his moral standard recognizes that what is involved is not the observance of one rite more or one less, but the very substance of human life—is man a being with a soul, or is he merely a verbal biped? If the fourth of the Ten Commandments ("Remember the Sabbath day to keep it holy") can be rejected, why should the sixth ("Thou shalt not murder") be any less subject to rejection?

Do-it-yourself moral systems seem to be popular at this moment. "It may be wrong for you, but it's not necessarily wrong for him" is the justification for any form of conduct (as noted in an earlier essay). This argument is usually employed to legitimize a mere indulgence, but it is also used to justify violence, including murder. It seems that there is a Gresham's Law operating in morality—the bad drives out the good. In the 1920's an Auschwitz was unthinkable. But is it unthinkable in the 1970's? Even worse than the possibility of another Holocaust is the difficulty some men have in branding it evil. "To kill may be wrong for you, but . . . "

The authority behind the Ten Commandments is cited in the opening line of the First Commandment: "I am the L-rd." G-d alone can command, "Thou shalt not murder." This same imperative includes also the commandment which calls upon us to observe the Sabbath. If we reserve the right to reject the Fourth Commandment because Sabbath observance does not conform with the "realities" of some society, then the Sixth and Seventh—"Thou shalt not murder" and "Thou shalt not commit adultery"—will inevitably meet the same fate because some day these, too, will be viewed as running counter to the "realities" of a given social group.

The Torah holds that man is a free agent whose moral decisions are autonomous. Providence does not impose moral decisions on man. "Everything is in the hands of heaven," the Talmud (*Berachot* 33b) declares, "excepting the fear of heaven." Cruelty and kindness alike are equally part of man's potential. G-d did not act to prevent Cain from practicing his form of brotherhood. But this does not mean that G-d was indifferent to what man does.

"Where are you?" G-d demanded of Adam after the first man had disobeyed G-d's command in the Garden of Eden. He asks the same question of every man, and each man has his own response, depending on his way of life. But how is man to make his decisions? On what basis shall he decide what is the good life and what is corrupt? Here, man could make a bitter, but justified retort to G-d.

"You ask where I am? I am right where You put me—in a world of confusion, without any guidance. You want me to be 'good', but You have not told me what 'good' is. My own mind cannot tell me, neither can all my science, nor can the society in which I live."

It is for this reason—to give man a resource, one superior to his own inadequate resources—that G-d has told man what is "life and what is death, what is good and what is evil." This is why the Torah was needed.

G-d wants to prevent bloodshed; He therefore declared, "Thou shalt not murder." He did not say, "Thou shalt study science," or paint pictures, or listen to symphonies, or build great empires. Such things will not wean man from his capacity for violence. Only man's acceptance of Torah can tell us where Eichmann was wrong.

G-d could have acted to keep Auschwitz from happening. However—and what I am about to say is *not* an attempt at explaining the Holocaust but simply an effort to articulate what we may learn from Auschwitz—if G-d had indeed done so, then man would have asserted that it was the human mind, the human spirit or human civilization which prevented the Holocaust, that man has no need for G-d. If man is to be truly free, then he must be free to make his own moral decisions, accepting or rejecting a given absolute moral standard, or else he is neither free nor even human.

Man's freedom lies in his ability to *choose* between good and evil, not in his capacity to *define* what is right and wrong. Auschwitz is a horror only by a certain definition. If our man-made definition and Eichmann's disagree, what is there to make our definition more compelling than his? In the final analysis, we must appeal to some standard higher than our own, or Eichmann's. You and I and Eichmann and society and science are *not* omniscient. There are problems that exceed our ability to deal with them. Auschwitz may not tell us anything about G-d, but it does tell us everything about man, and only Auschwitz could teach us that.

May I suggest that Auschwitz—and Auschwitz alone— demonstrated the infinite depths to which man can sink, depths incredible in a civilized world. Man's reliance on himself as the measure of all things could have remained intact—except for Auschwitz. Men had persuaded themselves that humanity had outgrown barbarism—until Auschwitz. Until Auschwitz, men were confident that they could chart the course of life without supernatural intervention, without revealed codes of law and still create a viable and moral society. But after Auschwitz, the conviction that man knows right from wrong was dispelled as a baseless illusion. Man must look outside himself for values, for morals, now that he has realized his inescapable limitations. Moral relativism was revealed to be bankrupt, useless in giving firm guidance. Had some miracle happened to avert Auschwitz, man could have attributed it to his own virtue, or to nature, and continued to insist on his own natural probity and moral self-sufficiency. He could have continued to insist that Torah might have been necessary in an earlier, barbaric age, but that it is redundant today when reason and intellect have advanced so far and become so infallible.

Auschwitz has shown the potential baseness of man; Torah teaches us his potential heights. The degeneracy of Auschwitz cannot be comprehended except through personal experience. By the same token it is true that the heights attainable through Torah ideals transcend our conventional conceptions of man and his nature. Man's capacity for selflessness, idealism, sublime feelings, refinement of thought—let us call it man's capacity for G-dliness—can only be imagined through experience.

The question, then, is not *which* morality should be adopted, but whether there is *any* morality at all. The question is not, "Is Shabbos really necessary?" but, "Is Auschwitz really wrong?"—and these two questions are not unrelated to one another.

Revelation

Any discussion of the authority of Torah rests ultimately on whether we accept Torah as the revealed word of G-d, rather than the product of human efforts. The contemporary mind is not at ease with such concepts as Divine revelation or the Divine authorship of a book. Books, we know quite well, are written by men. Why should this one Book be different?

Parenthetically, we might consider this point in assessing the claims of the Bible critics. Assume for the moment that there were no "contradictions" or discrepancies whatsoever within the Five Books of Moses, that it would be obvious to anyone that the entire *Chumash* is the work of one hand. Whose hand, we ask the Bible critics, might that be? G-d's? The Bible critic would hardly agree. The author must have been Moses, or some other man. The Bible critics' rejection of Torah as G-d's document is not a consequence of their analysis. They started out from the premise that the Bible is the work of mortals, and then they proceeded to marshal evidence to refute arguments against their assumption.

Revelation is an elusive concept—insubstantial, unpalpable, unfamiliar to our common human experience. Small wonder that men should shy away from confronting the concept. They try to evade it by bland euphemisms such as describing the Torah as an "inspired" document. But this does not resolve the problem. Shakespeare was probably "inspired," too, but this does not, and should not, instill in us the moral compulsion to emulate his ways. Virtually everything "good" in this world could be described as "inspired." After all, man's intelligence—indeed, all that exists—comes from G-d. By describing the Torah as "revelation" we declare that to follow Torah is to follow G-d's will, and that to ignore Torah is to violate the will of the Creator. No one ever claimed that Shakespeare was enunciating the will of G-d in his writings.

We are dealing with a "religious" category; we use this term to describe a relationship between man and G-d, and behavior that tends to cement, or to sunder, that relationship. We are not at this moment concerned with esthetics or utilitarian values, but with G-d and man. Both Beethoven and physics may be moving and impressive, stirring man to an awareness of something beyond and greater than himself, but artists and scientists alike may resolutely insist that their works are not "religious." The studio and laboratory are not "houses of worship"; the undoubtedly spiritual effects which they may, and frequently do, generate are not the primary or direct results of their efforts.

Another parenthetical remark to avoid possible misunderstanding. Torah does indeed emphasize the universal character of the religious experience—"In all your ways, know Him!" One can transmute an ordinary experience like eating, or doing business, or engaging in sports, into something spiritualizing. Here a "neutral" act becomes sanctified, just as a symphony or mathematical formula can give rise to sublime emotions, even religious emotions. The "religious" experience by contrast, is not in need of transmutation. Prayer and charity do not start out as "neutral."

To return to our original problem, the Divine authorship of the Torah. "Can you prove it?" is the demand thrown at the traditionalists. There is an abundance of arguments and proofs, more or less convincing—as often less as more. The discussion may become quite heated, but as a rule it is sterile. When the storm has subsided, we usually find the participants in the debate unchanged in their views. Those who are already convinced do not need to be persuaded; the·skeptical are not amenable to persuasion. Perhaps some other approach will yield up a more appropriate response to the challenge, "Can you prove it?" Let us see just what proof would be acceptable when it comes to a discussion of this question.

If you announce that you have found a cure for the common cold, the standard of proof is obvious. If you claim that you can change lead into gold, someone will hand you a lump of lead to see whether you can transform it. But if you should propose that the Torah was given by G-d, how can you prove your statement? Try the Torah itself. The Torah says that it was given by G-d. But is that enough to convince your questioner? Let's try another approach. My teacher told me that the Torah was given by G-d. How did he know? Because his own teacher told him so, and so forth, through the generations, all the way back to Sinai. "Are you still not convinced?" you ask your questioner. "You are not? Then *you* tell me what you would accept as proof that the Torah was given by G-d."

A "valid" challenge or question is one that is amenable to solution. A question which, by its very nature, cannot be answered is not "valid." If, by the very definition of the concept, we cannot "prove" the Divine authorship of the Torah, then the demand for proof is not valid. Discussions may be stimulating and sparkling but they will be fruitless just the same. Instead of seeking a proof of revelation, I suggest that we keep the question in abeyance and explore other facets of revelation.

"Assuming, just for argument's sake," a young student once asked at an Encounter, "that G-d did indeed speak to Moses. But even then, the words of G-d were written down by Moses, a fallible mortal. Isn't it likely that in the process the text of the Torah was changed, so that what we now have is not the original revealed document at all, but one that bears the impress of a human mind?" *Chassidus,* drawing as it generally does from earlier sources, has an answer to the student's question.

The Torah is divided into two parts, the Written Law (set down in the Hebrew Bible) and the Oral Law (which was revealed to Moses on Mount Sinai at the same time as the

Written Law, and was only set down in the Talmud centuries later). Both Laws were given by G-d, but while the Written Law was "dictated" by G-d to Moses word for word, the verbalization of the Oral Law was less precise. The text of the Written Law, from the very beginning, was recopied by scribes, word for word. The Oral Law, on the other hand, was transmitted by word of mouth one generation to another, just as it had been communicated orally by G-d Himself to Moses, with less concern for verbal precision. In the Written Law the *word* is crucial; in the Oral Law, *ideas* are the more important factor. A Torah scroll with so much as one word, or one letter, incorrect, is not "kosher." Such strictures do not apply to the Oral Law.

Words, or, in Chassidic usage, "letters," are vehicles for ideas. The "word" is inert, static, precise. A word dictated by one person to another is the same word, unchanged no matter who repeats it. When we are told that the Written Law was "dictated" verbatim by G-d, we are to understand that Moses wrote down the words as he heard them, without any change or modification. In a sense, Moses was simply the first one of many scribes, all of whom performed the same function, that of recording the Written Law as they heard, or saw it, word for word.

The situation is different in the case of the Oral Law, where the emphasis is on ideas. Since one idea can be presented in many different ways, one thinker may select one set of words and his colleague another. One thinker may be succinct, the other verbose. Here, the personality of the speaker is evident in his choice of words, and even the idea may be subtly modified by the choice of expressions used. Of course, word and idea are not separate, but for our purposes it is important to remember the difference in emphasis: the Oral Law stresses the *idea*; the Written Law accentuates the role of the *word*. Thus, it is considered a *mitzvah* to recite the Psalms even if one does not understand what he is reciting. Rote recitation of Talmudic passages, on the other hand, is a sheer waste of time, because in the Oral Law the idea is dominant and the word secondary. The Oral Law demands that we understand it; the Written Law, by contrast, defies ultimate understanding.

(Maimonides said that every word recorded in the Written Law is sacred. Thus, the passage in which Timnah is described as the concubine of Eliphaz, son of Esau (Gen. 36:12) is considered no less holy than the *Sh'ma* (Deut. 6:4-9) or the statement, "I am the L-rd your G-d" (Exodus 20:2), which introduces the Ten Commandments. Our inability to understand the Written Torah creates what we consider anomalies like this statement of Maimonides. While interpretations like Midrash and *Kabbalah* offer another stratum of meaning, apart from the literal, the Bible remains an ultimate mystery. We pronounce the words but cannot grasp the ideas.)

The point here is that Moses did not verbalize the Torah which G-d dictated to him. He did not verbalize a vision. The Torah was revealed to him in the form of words, so that his role was a passive one. He was the scribe, not the communicator of ideas.

How did G-d communicate with Moses? Unfortunately, this is another doomed speculation. We shall never know, at least not until G-d, or Moses tells us. It was a one-time event, truly unique. We have no similar experience in our history to draw upon. But, Torah doctrine states that regardless of the means employed by G-d to reveal His words to Moses, He communicated his revelation in the form of *words*.

How did the revelation at Sinai actually take place? Basically this question is similar to the one about G-d's communicating the Torah to Moses. The answer would also be the same; we simply do not and cannot know. But speculation can be pleasant. Suppose someone had had a tape recorder at Mount Sinai. Would it have recorded G-d's voice proclaiming, "I am the L-rd . . . "? Was the revelation an oral-aural experience, a "voice" in the literal, physical sense of the word, measurable by sound waves? Or was it a revelation of some other order? It is better to present the question than to pretend to resolve it. Whatever took place at Sinai was unparalleled, unique, not comparable to anything that we might be able to comprehend from our own limited experience.

* * * * * *

We suggested at the outset that attempts to prove Divine revelation are sterile unless there is agreement on what would be considered a valid proof. The initial burden of defining "proof" would properly lie with the one who demands such proof. Otherwise we will find ourselves in an interminable struggle against arbitrary and fluctuating standards. Or, instead of being merely frustrated by an intrinsic inadequacy in the proposed proof, we will simply find ourselves unable to accept the concept of revelation.

Obviously, there are some who may not have articulated their conceptions of what, in their eyes, would constitute a valid proof. They have not yet formulated their standards, but the very fact that they are questing, that they are open to persuasion, shows that they have not rejected the authenticity of the Torah out of hand.

Of course, there is no objection to seeking proofs for G-d's existence, for Divine revelation, or any other religious tenet, for that matter. The point we wish to make is merely that in questions of religion, the criteria for proof are not the same as those that can be applied to science or history.

On one occasion, a student offered a specific challenge. "Point to one statement in the Torah which was vindicated by subsequent historical events and which could not possibly have been composed by a human mind.

Let us look for a passage that would meet this requirement.

Thirty-five centuries ago, kings were not particularly inhibited by humility. If we are to believe the chronicles left of their reigns, none of them ever lost a war. These potentates were no ordinary kings; they described themselves as "kings of kings" who modestly compared the sun's brilliance with their own, and found the sun wanting. Their wealth was beyond reckoning and their military power beyond challenge. The rulers of ancient Egypt, Assyria, and Persia boasted that their empires would be eternal, something along the lines of the thousand-year Reich of Adolf Hitler.

The *Chumash,* the Five Books of Moses, the record of the early history of the Jewish people, represents a complete departure from these other chronicles. Moses does not glorify the Children of Israel and their leaders. Instead, he chastises his people not only for the sins they committed in the past, but also for those which they would commit in the future. He glowingly describes the land which G-d promised to the Israelites, but then foretells in chilling words the destruction of that beautiful land, the dispersion of the Jews, and the incredible sufferings they would have to endure in exile. All chronicles were replete with predictions of future glory; only the Torah gave a preview of Israel's future humiliation. Could all this have been the work of a mere mortal, even one of the stature of Moses?

Some might explain all this by suggesting that Moses had some kind of prescience—though there is no reason why even such a possibility should be taken for granted. But then, how is one to explain—even now that it has proven true beyond question—the prediction that despite all its sufferings, Israel will survive?

When the Babylonians destroyed Jerusalem, it seemed that Israel's day was done. When Rome destroyed the Holy City a second time some five centuries later, it appeared obvious to all, once again, that Israel was doomed. The destruction of Jerusalem was followed by 2,000 years of exile, an indescribable succession of expulsions and wanderings, the pogroms, and finally that ultimate horror which no other people could have survived, the Hitler holocaust. Is there a Jew alive today with a heart so shriveled that he doubts the eternity of Israel? All honor to Moses, but no human being could ever have predicted what he did, and with such accuracy. I would suggest that it is easier to believe in the existence of G-d and in Divine revelation than it is to believe that Moses, an ordinary mortal, could have been the author of the *tochechah,* the "chapters of reproof" (Lev. 26:14–45 and Deut. 28:15–68), which so graphically predict the exile of the Jewish people.

This, then, might be proposed as one response to the challenge to prove the Divine character of the Torah. Here is a preview of future history that no human being could have written. *If* this proposed standard of proof is considered acceptable by the questioner, then "proof" is hereby offered.

The *fact* of Sinai—that our ancestors stood there, saw the cloud, beheld the lightning and thunder, heard the blast of the *shofar* and the proclamation, "I am the L-rd your G-d"—is not the issue here. The persuasive factors are the unbroken survival of the tradition, and the circumstance that all of Israel, not just Moses alone, experienced the revelation on the mountain the wilderness. The Children of Israel had no compunctions about challenging Aaron's priesthood or even the authority and mission of Moses. One need only recall the clamor of the Israelites for the fleshpots of Egypt, and the mass adoration of the Golden Calf. But none of the Israelites ever questioned Moses' account of what had happened on Mount Sinai. This acceptance of Divine revelation by an entire generation should certainly impress the skeptic.

But there remains one troubling question. When Israel heard a voice proclaiming, "I am the L-rd your G-d," *whose* voice did they hear? How did they know that it really was the voice of G-d? This is the challenge to Divine revelation that we are attempting to discuss here. Ultimately the challenge is a subjective one. "Can you prove it to *me*?" Here again, if he expects a serious answer, the questioner must propose standards of acceptable proof.

Some hold that revelation cannot be subjected to proof, in the ordinary sense. It was a unique, one-time event that has no points of comparison with any other human experience. It must therefore be accepted as a matter of *ani ma'amin,* of "I believe" with a "perfect faith," independent of proof or demonstration. Any argument against it would be irrelevant.

We frequently collide with that scornful expression, "*blind faith,*" as noted earlier in the essay, "EMUNAH." Faith, as the Torah teaches it, and particularly in the case of Divine revelation, is not something for which apologies are necessary. The mind has arrived at an impasse. It cannot deal with this subject, but this is no reason to dismiss the matter out of hand as being anti-rational, as doing violence to reason. Can reason accept the idea of Divine revelation, the proposition that G-d can, and does, communicate with man? To the believer, reason is no obstacle to the acceptance of Revelation, while his faith enables him to accept it.

Let us explore this subject a little further.

Any talk about revelation of necessity involves faith. Now faith implies a negation, or lack of reason, and who wants to be irrational, mindless? A word is in order about faith and reason, or as the Hebrew puts is, *emunah* and *sechel*. Can a rational being possess faith, without compartmentalizing himself, without turning off his mind when ever he opens the *Siddur*? Is the "thinking believer" a contradiction, a split personality?

Reason is demonstrable, dimensioned and finite. Aside from the simple limitations of ignorance (not all of us read Sanskrit or understand the theory of relativity) and contemporary horizons of knowledge (the questions scientists still ask with no answers in sight) that restrict mankind as a whole, the human intellect is subject to intrinsic limitations. We are physical beings, and hence subject to the limits of matter. Our minds can handle the dimensioned, the finite, and speak of the infinite. But we cannot really understand the truly infinite. Time and space set boundaries, not only for our bodies but also for our minds. We cannot conceive of a situation transcending time, where past, present and future not only merge, but don't even exist. "Here" and "there" are distinct concepts; they are nonexistent for the infinite.

The limits of reason are limits for nothing *but* reason. They do not limit reality. Whatever we do not, or cannot, understand may be true just the same, and our inability to understand it is due simply to a lack within ourselves. The transcendent may well exist, whether we understand it or not. (We have obviously not "proven" its existence, but there is a *possibility* that it exists, and that is enough for the moment.) Only an irrational conceit will refuse to admit the possible existence of anything beyond human capacities and experience.

How do we deal with these supradimensionals? Here we come to the province of faith. Faith works where reason cannot function. (Note: this does not imply that reason is *contrary* to faith.) Man can now deal with more than the dimensional, more than the observable, with more than what he has experienced and is capable of duplicating. The "instrument" with which he can accomplish this is faith.

It must be emphasized that faith is not an appeal to the irrational, the contra-rational. Faith is not isolated from reason or arbitrary in its pronouncements or assumptions. It is part of a continuum that includes intellect and emotion, and is engaged only when the intellect proves incompetent. Reason leads us to the outer frontiers of dimension; faith extends man's reach to the undimensioned. Faith is built on reason, not bounded by it. Where reason is extended, faith becomes redundant. What I accepted yesterday on faith, because I could not understand, I accept today by reason, because I am able to understand it now.

Revelation, the soul, the World To Come, the *Moshiach*—these are only a few instances of concepts requiring *emunah*, faith. They do not run counter to reason. They do no violence to intellect, but they have no proofs. Let us return to the first concept we named, Revelation. At the outset we offer several premises, some noted in earlier essays, some logical, some artibrary but, we hope, acceptable. With these assumptions, revelation becomes part of a pattern, symmetrical and logical.

The first premise concerns the nature of man. Man is

not—to put it in dogmatic, categorical terms—merely a higher form of animal life. He is even something more than a creature that can devise gadgets to help him walk on the moon or transplant hearts. Man is in "the image of G-d." There is more to man than the visible, physical body, more than the mind that controls aspects of the physical. Man is unique, because man alone is capable of making moral decisions. Man is free because having been created "in the image" of his Creator, he is under no compulsions. This moral quality of life, this differentiation between good and evil, is the human element of, if you wish, the divine within man, as distinct from the "animal" within him.

What is the extent of this freedom? Man is not free to *determine* good and evil, but he has been given the freedom to choose between the two, as discussed in the essay, "Holocaust."

Our second premise is that the resources at man's disposal are insufficient to define morality. We might describe several resources; others suggested would no doubt be no more impressive.

a) *Reason.* After millenia of endeavor to define what is "good" and "the good life," philosophers seem to have despaired of being able to arrive at a definitive formulation. From the viewpoint of logic, "Thou shalt *not* steal" and "thou *shalt* steal" are equally valid—or equally irrelevant. The moral statement needs some foundation, one which reason alone cannot provide. We are not prepared to say that since reason does not lead to a moral definition, morality does not exist. At least I hope that no one will say it, though sometimes the human experience makes one wonder . . .

b) *Society.* "Is it right or wrong?"

"It may be wrong for you, but it may be all right for someone else."

"Even shooting an innocent passer-by?"

"Well, you may feel it's wrong, but someone else, etc . . . "

That is a verbatim reconstruction of a conversation I had

with some students. Something may be "wrong" in one society but entirely acceptable in another. It is the society that determines whether a given pattern of behavior is good or evil. The inference is drawn that all morality is "situational," "relative" and subjective.

Is morality purely a societal function? Then why should anyone submit to the arbitrary decrees of society? Hasn't almost all human progress been stimulated by the nonconformists?

c) *Science.* Since it deals only with the observable, the quantitative and the tangible, science is not qualified to enter the argument over morality. "Good" cannot be observed or measured with a radiotelescope or an electronic microscope. The scientist's personal moral predilections may be pronounced and admirable, but this does not make them "science."

d) *Human nature.* Some still believe in the essential humanity of man. They are convinced that man is engaged in a never-ceasing ascent up the ladder of decency. In this view, the excesses of Tamerlane and Genghis Khan are part of ancient history, never to be repeated. This Pollyanna faith in man's goodness could be acceptable in 1930, but not to the generation that has been blessed with Auschwitz.

True, it isn't too much trouble to devise a "moral" system, a thoroughly satisfying one that will appeal to all our higher instincts and strivings, but there will always be someone else who will propose a different code, just as valid though diametrically opposed. The decision as to which of the two is the ideal one comes from elsewhere. Neither code is imperative, so neither can dictate restraint when indulgence is so delightful.

The third premise concerns G-d and His intentions. He placed man in the material world, and endowed him with the ability to choose the good in preference to evil so that he will be able to transcend his gross physical nature. Without Divine guidance man does not know, and is incapable of ever finding out what the "good" is.

Let's see what we might speculate about G-d.

G-d is great, so great that He can care about one single puny person among four billion others—even one act, one word, one thought of that person. That's how big G-d is. He is not limited to or by the cosmos. If, therefore, someone asks whether G-d really cares about trifles, the answer is that whatever concerns a human being is never a mere trifle. The uniqueness of man, the spiritual element expressed in his ability to act independently, his description as the "image of G-d," gives particular importance to every aspect of his being. Man is not just a quantity, to be evaluated in terms of one out of four billion. Man is an infinity; there are four billion infinities, if you will, walking the earth this very morning, and none of these infinities impinges on any of the others. It seems to me entirely proper that the Infinite cares about the infinite.

The common challenge to *mitzvot* involves the question whether the so-called ritual *mitzvot* are binding. Why concern ourselves with whether or not we are allowed to switch on a light on Shabbos? Isn't it enough to be a decent person? The implication of these questions is that G-d cares about whether we obey the commandment, "Thou shalt not steal," but that it is a matter of indifference to Him whether or not we put on *tefillin*. The social *mitzvot* are more acceptable, to our minds.

We propose that a One-to-one relationship between G-d and man is not demeaning to Him. How can we confine His interest in man to the plural, to the social virtues, and insist that the personal life of the individual is not part of G-d's concern? In the symbiotic relationship between the two elements of man, the outer, public man is a reflection of the inward. A person who is inwardly corrupt, self-indulgent, arrogant and undisciplined cannot be selfless and idealistic in his public life. According to those who would discount the concept of mitzvah, I as an individual am of no account except if I am with someone else, I assume value and importance in the eyes of G-d only when I am together with another. The Torah dismisses this notion out of hand.

But we are beginning to digress. The significance of the mitzvah is another, albeit critical, matter to be dealt with another time. It is enough at this moment to state that G-d is concerned with guiding men not only as a group but also as individuals.

Here is faith, the complement of reason. Reason demonstrates its own limitations, its incompetence in the realm of the moral, indicating that the moral is supra-rational. We state, perhaps dogmatically but not unreasonably, that man's existence has a definite purpose, namely, the realization of his potential, the ability of making the values of the intangible spiritual superior to those of the immediate, the fleshly, the "animal." We further declare that just as G-d "does not play dice with the universe" He does not play dice with man. He has created man and He guides him; in other words, *He reveals His Will to man.* Revelation, then, is only a logical link in a succession.

Faith is not some blind leap over—or into—a chasm. There is an almost measurable relationship between dictates of reason and declarations of faith; where the mind stops because it can go no further, faith comes forth to make its contribution to man's perspective of self, world, and Creator. Nor is faith the escape of the weakling who lacks in intellectual or moral fibre. Faith, in our view, is an extension of man's faculties, proceeding from the observable and demonstrable to the less tangible, from intellect to faith.

* * * * * *

What is the special relationship of the Jew to the Revelation at Sinai? Granted that G-d would not leave man without guidance, aren't there any number of so-called "revelations" vying for human sould, each proclaiming itself the One True Faith?

It is not our purpose to embark upon a voyage through comparative religion or upon analyses of different faiths. All we seek to do is simply to explore the claim of Sinai to our allegiance.

Let us start at the beginning—at Bereshis, Genesis. G-d created a world, placed a man upon it, and told him how to live. Man was not obedient for very long—the first generation of man committed the prototype of all sins, and later generations were quick to learn. As soon as there were two brothers, there was one murderer. From then on, things steadily became worse, until finally the corruption became too much to bear, or to cure, and a flood was sent to cleanse the earth. But even this apparently did not impress mankind sufficiently to mend its ways. Here and there a solitary light glimmered, a lonely man of faith and goodness, largely ignored, apparently quite ineffectual. Twenty generations had elapsed since the days of Adam but mankind had hardly progressed.

Then one man appeared who all by himself discovered the concept of G-d, not just as Creator but as a G-d Who expects man to fulfill certain expectations. This man was not content with his own saintliness (he was, in fact, unaware that he had any virtues at all), but he knew that he must share whatever he possessed. He proceeded to "convert" men to belief in G-d, while his wife, Sarah, taught the women. He lived a long life of ceaseless work. He had eight sons and we might expect that he lavished care upon them. He wanted them, also, to live "in G-d's presence," to be aware of G-d, His closeness permeating their lives, to know that their every trivial act should bear the impress of G-d's concern. Abraham, the Torah tells us, taught righteousness and justice to his children. But how many of his own sons did he manage to convince? Only one. But this was enough, for through this one son, the values taught by Abraham could be passed on to the next generation. There now was a chance that these values could be perpetuated.

The life of this son, Isaac, was marked by sacrifice. Isaac in turn had two sons, but again, only one son, Jacob, chose to emulate his father. But there were three generations now, a triple strand of strength and permanence. What was to be a fitting reward for Abraham, Isaac and Jacob? G-d granted them the only reward a moral person desires, the

one reward which has true meaning for Jewish parents—
the blessing of having good children, children who will
guide themselves by the laws of G-d, who will treat others
as they should be treated, who will live their personal lives
in character with the "image of G-d" in which they were
created. Abraham struggled for his faith. Isaac was ready to
lay down his life upon the sacrificial altar for *his* faith. The
faith of Jacob was tested by Esau and Lavan. From then on,
the survival of the values proclaimed by Abraham was no
longer in doubt. All of Jacob's children followed in his
path. What was not granted to Abraham and Isaac was
given to Jacob. The spark generated by the Fathers had
been endowed the children.

But what of all the rest of humanity, those who are not
members of the covenant of Abraham? They too, know
what G-d requires of them. G-d told it to Adam, and he
told it to Noah. Man must not steal, murder, blaspheme,
commit adultery, worship idols, or torture animals. It is
expected of him to set up courts of justice to defend the
defenseless. If everyone observed this simple code, we
would have utopia.

How should we pray? Which is the "true" religion? The
Torah gives the non-Jew almost unbounded latitude. All
that is expected of him is that he remain within the
framework of the "Seven Commandments of the Sons of
Noah." G-d cares about *all* men, no matter what their
religion, and whether they observe or violate the Seven
Commandments is not a matter of indifference to Him.
These Seven Commandments blaze a trail for man to move
closer to G-d; whoever violates them creates a chasm between himself and his Creator.

But the Seven Commandments have only a limited influence on everyday life. They do not demand constant vigi-
lance. We are not *always* tempted to kill, or to steal. Religion
based only on the Noah commandments is unobtrusive.
This was not enough for Abraham. It was his desire—and
that of his son, and of his grandson—to dwell in the presence of G-d at all times, to have constant communication

with Him, not just at the elementary seven points of contact. G-d acceded to Abraham's wish. At Sinai, G-d formalized His covenant with Abraham's descendants. He taught them how live "in His presence" at all times, how to make even the transactions of everyday business a form of worship, how to make marriage a covenant with G-d.

The Revelation at Sinai, then, is the climactic experience of Israel, the culmination of generations of struggle against temptations within and a hostile environment without. The Revelation at Sinai speaks to the Jew with a unique claim and relevance. When G-d proclaimed the Seven Commandments His word was directed to all men. When He proclaimed the Torah, He addressed himself to one particular segment of mankind—the Jews.

Of course, any man, no matter what his origin or his present religion (or irreligion), who, like Abraham, seeks to live constantly in the presence of G-d, is free to take upon himself the additional commitment which Abraham and his descendants took upon themselves—he can adopt Judaism. By *giyur k'halacha,* conversion in accordance with Torah law, he too can become *ben Avraham Avinu,* a true son of Abraham.

But this is not expected of the Gentile if he does not wish to do so. He may be spiritually satisfied with the occasional contact with G-d as embodied in the Seven Laws of Noah.

Not so the Jew. For him, his Jewishness is inherent. The commitment implied in the covenant of Abraham is not something he may choose or reject at will. It is part of his very being.

Tefillin Today

(This essay was originally delivered at the Bar Mitzvah celebration of Israel's war orphans in Kfar Chabad, on 12 Tammuz 1970, and then adapted for print for an English-speaking audience.)

The Six-Day war brought a rejuvenation of *tefillin* observance all over the world. Special impetus for this revival came forth from the Wall.* *Tefillin* is a distinctively Jewish way of worship; it is the central mitzvah with which boys are initiated into Jewish manhood. It represents an act rather than a sentiment or a word. But what, you may ask, is the message of *tefillin* for our own day?

The threat confronting civilization today is not rhetorical. Acts of violence are real and increasing in both frequency and intensity. Not too long ago, the university, that exemplar of rationality, turned out to be a hotbed of terror. Professors of philosophy, graduate students, some of the finest minds America has cultivated, engaged in indiscriminate violence, using guns and bombs. Violence as such is nothing new, but that people of learning should engage in it *is* something new—and deeply disturbing.

It is worthy of note that the first direct quotation from Moses in the Torah is his protest against a Jew who had raised his arm to strike another. "Why do you strike your fellow?" Moses is introduced to us as a protester against an act of violence.

What do the *tefillin* symbolize? The straps are wrapped around the arms. As a result, the arm loses its freedom of

---

*The Western Wall in Jerusalem, where visitors are encouraged to put on *tefillin*, often for the first time in their lives.

movement; it can only move as the straps permit. Man is not free to do as he wishes. He can move his arm—that is, he can use his ability to act—only in ways that are in consonance with the spirit of the *tefillin,* of the *Sh'ma.* Some acts, such as taking that which belongs to another, or harming a fellow man or an animal, or even willfully damaging inanimate objects, are evil. Arms and hands have the power to heal and help, to create and build, and they must be used only for these purposes. This is what the *tefillin* tell us each morning, and the Bar Mitzvah youth enters life, just as we ourselves enter it anew each day, with the reminder that all our actions must be in character with these principles.

One box of our *tefillin* is placed upon the left arm, near the heart, symbolically the seat of our emotions. There are certain emotions which the Torah prohibits. "Do not hate your brother in your heart," for hatred is a sin. "Do not harbor a grudge," even when you have been wronged. "You shall love the stranger" with all his alienness, and certainly, "you shall love your fellow as yourself." Our emotions are not beyond our control. We are responsible for our emotions. We are to be their master, not their pawn. This is another message that our *tefillin* hold for us today.

The *tefillin* give us a glimpse of the magnificent potential inherent in every one of us, not only to *do* what is right, but also to remain in control of our emotions. That common but feeble excuse, "I couldn't help myself," is not acceptable to anyone sensitive to the message of the *tefillin.* A heart touched by the *tefillin* and fired with the command to "love your G-d with all your heart" will reject such pettiness.

The other box of the *tefillin* is placed upon the head, the seat of the mind. Man's mind is his finest gift and at the same time the most ominous threat to the world in which he lives. If he uses his mind properly, he can create a paradise; if he does not, he can bring utter destruction to the planet. He must use his mind in accordance with the teachings of the Torah, his thoughts must be pure, he must not plot and scheme against others, and he must not utilize his brain for self-aggrandizement at the expense of others. Almost everyone in the Western world today is able to read and write, but when it comes to moral literacy we are still scarcely beyond the caveman stage. The educated but immoral are not governed by their intellect; their minds are enslaved by their base instincts. The *tefillin* declare to us that the mind must have direction; lacking such direction, it can lead man to his ruin.

The Torah tells us to place our *tefillin* "between the eyes." How we use our eyes shows what sort of people we are. When the late Lubavitcher Rebbe was still a little boy, he asked his father why G-d gave man two eyes. Would not one eye have been quite sufficient? "G-d gave us two eyes, a right eye and a left eye," his father replied. "The right eye is for seeing the good, and the left eye is for seeing faults. Use your right eye to look at others, and your left eye to look at yourself."

Tefillin are a bond and a "sign" binding the American Jew, the Soviet Jew and the Israeli Jew together into one inseparable whole, and at the same time tying the hand, the mind and the heart of the Jew to G-d and Torah, to ideal and principle. These qualities are not found in abundance today . . .

The idea of *tefillin* binding the individual to his people needs elaboration. Not all Jews today are as blessed as we are, free to observe the tenets of Torah. Today a community numbering millions of Jews is forbidden to teach its young the heritage of Torah. A boy of 13 often cannot get a pair of *tefillin*. The sanctions of a mighty and determined state are enforced to bar the Jew from his faith; religious loyalty may result in imprisonment and exile.

We want to demonstrate our concern for these Jews, our oneness with them in their plight. What they cannot teach, we must learn and transmit. What they cannot do to perpetuate Judaism, we must do for them. What they cannot keep, we must cherish and nurture.

Tefillin can be such a demonstration. The young Jew in

Russia is not permitted to wear *tefillin*; therefore, the young Jew here in Israel and wherever we are free must wear *tefillin*, for both of them. We have no delusions about the state of *Yiddishkeit* today; we know that the number of those who do not yet observe *tefillin* is exceedingly large. But we also know that the young Jew is concerned about the "Jews of Silence." *Tefillin* offers the young Jew a way in which he can speak for, and to, the Jews of Russia, and to the future, proclaiming that nothing can crush the eternity of our Torah. The student here in Israel will wear *tefillin* for the student in Russia who cannot, and with every twist of the strap around his arm, he is bound closer to the fate of his people. The *tefillin* strap spans oceans and continents, binding a scattered people into one strong unit.

An awesome picture—a barracks in Auschwitz, and inside it a line of Jews, hurriedly putting on a single secret pair of *tefillin*, then taking them off again at once without a chance to recite the *Sh'ma,* because the Germans could come in at any moment. While some of the inmates put on the *tefillin*, others stationed themselves at the barracks door to watch out for the Nazis. A member of my Congregation was in that group.

And then another picture appears before my mind—a line of thousands of Jewish students stretching for blocks around a Hillel House at a large American university, waiting for an opportunity to put on *tefillin,* unhurried, and without fear ... Is it fantasy? Is there a better way of demonstrating that the Jew who is free cares about his brothers—wherever they may be?

Why Mitzvot?

"Why should I observe Shabbos or put on *tefillin*?" This question is the inevitable reaction whenever the mitzvot are discussed. The question might go beyond the simple "why"; it may reach into intellectual difficulties, problems involved in theoretical commitment and practical observance, conflicting claims on the individual's present life and loyalties. Sooner or later, the scornful point out, we will revert to an apparently helpless appeal to the inscrutable, infinite wisdom of G-d, an appeal which they regard as a cop-out, an evasion of real issues.

There are two forms of questioning that emerge when *mitzvah* observance is discussed, and they should be kept apart. First: why did G-d command us to do, or not to do, such-and-such? Second: what will observing the mitzvah do for *me*? Will it make me a better person?

Let us take the two forms of questioning in turn.

A popular question, also discussed in the essay, "Speak English . . ." is why the Torah should forbid the eating of certain kinds of meat. With a gleam in his eyes as if he had suddenly made a startling original discovery, the questioner will patiently proceed to explain that in the "olden days" people did not have the sanitation, government inspection, and refrigeration that exist today, don't you see? In those days, the *kosher* laws made sense. But aren't they irrelevant today?

An ordinary layman might be excused for this superficial questioning. After all, he does not pretend to Jewish scholarship. But all too often this same argument is parroted by people who should know better. In the 11th century, Rashi, in his classic, universally accepted commentary on the *Chumash*, clearly and repeatedly declared (and he was quoting a Talmudic statement made many centuries before his own day) that the Biblical ban against eating pork was one of those prohibitions in the Torah for which there is no rational explanation. Had he considered it to be a "health measure," he would have included it among the "rational" laws, which we will discuss shortly, but he obviously did not view it as such.

Observers of human behavior seek to explain human patterns of conduct in terms of their underlying values and motivations, conscious and subconscious. This is reasonable because the observer and his subject are human. Both observer and subject may have similar cultural backgrounds; if not, then the observer should at least be familiar with his subject's background. The extent to which he acquires this knowledge will have an influence on the conclusions he draws. Some common ground between observer and subject is essential in enabling the former to find an explanation for the conduct of the latter. What the observer is saying in effect is, "If *I* were to behave like my subject, what would *my* motivation be?" If the subject's background is completely alien and unknown to the observer, and if the observer is unable to draw on his own previous experience with apparently universal human traits, it would be futile for the observer even to attempt to explain the motivations for his subject's values and behavior patterns.

This could apply also to a human "observer" who attempts to find the "motivations" for the laws of G-d. There is an infinite, unbridgeable gap between the intelligence of man and the wisdom of G-d. As Isaiah said, "Your thoughts are not like My thoughts." The human mind and experience are limited. No one mind can encompass the totality of human knowledge. The world of the unknown is infinite and constantly growing. The human capacity for thinking is limited by dimensions of time and space. We lack the ability to picture a Being who is everywhere at the same time, for Whom past, present, and future do not exist, for Whom, indeed, there is no time or space at all. We need not go into further detail on the limitations of the human intellect. The point we want to make is simply that the workings of the human mind are not, and can never be, comparable to the "processes" of the thoughts of G-d.

In attempting to find rationales for Torah and *mitzvot,* man in effect is saying, much like the scientist-observer, "If *I* made such a law, what would *my* motivation be? Why should anyone want to propose such ordinances? What meaning do these laws have for us?" The only thing wrong with this approach, when applied to the study of the Torah, is that the Torah was not proposed by "anyone," by a mind on a par with that of the questioner, but by an intellect beyond the limits of that of man. G-d's reasons for His mitzvot are beyond our powers of divination. His reasons are constant, unchanging, even as He Himself is not subject to change. It is only man's subjective appreciation of the mitzvot that varies.

In contrast to the question we have just described, the second form of questioning, "Why should *I* observe the *mitzvot?*" is perfectly legitimate and possibly answerable. Here rationalization is appropriate, because our question centers not on G-d but on man and his needs. What, you ask, will putting on *tefillin* do for me? Why should I refrain from driving on Shabbos, eat only kosher food, and *daven* three times each day? What are the effects of *mitzvah* observance? These questions can all be answered, and in fact, it is only proper to ask them, for once the Jew has found his answers, he will perform the *mitzvah* with more enthusiasm and spirit than before, and will be more sensitive to its effects. Torah is meant to be understood; blind obedience can be deceptive and superficial.

Before exploring a particular *mitzvah,* we must recognize several implications of this second form of questioning. Your answer, whatever it may be, is bound to be subjective, and there is—within reasonable limits, of course—no such thing as a "wrong" answer to the question, "Why should *I* keep the mitzvot?" *What* the Jew must do, and *how* he must do it, come under the heading of *Halacha,* of law, which by its very nature is objective and impersonal. On the other hand, the question *why* the Jew observes these laws, what significance they have for him, is subjective and the answer is not the same for every individual. Some may be led by sentiment; others may think in terms of Divine retribution; still others act out of respect for principles and ideals, or out of a sense of identification with Jewish history and the Jewish people. There is no doubt that personal motivations for *mitzvah* observance have changed as Jews have moved through time and across continents. Shabbos cannot have had the same personal significance for a Jew who lived in a peasant or shepherd society as it did for a Jew in the early cruel industrial age or as it does for a Jew in our own increasingly widespread leisure culture. For one Jew, Shabbos may be simply a day of rest from exhausting toil; for another, it may be an opportunity to study Torah; for a third, it may be a time for pleasant association with family and friends in a congenial Shabbos atmosphere. Perhaps Shabbos may be regarded as the sign that distinguished our own faith from that of others and this preserves the individuality of Judaism.

Let us go further. An explanation for a *mitzvah,* say candlelighting before Shabbos, which may seem entirely logical and convincing to a young girl may not impress her mother and grandmother, and vice versa. Considerations that appealed to me yesterday may not persuade me today, for all of us can, and should, grow in wisdom and sensitivity as we mature. Maimonides traces the process of maturation in the changing motivations that lead man to study the Torah in the course of his lifetime. At every stage of life the motivation is different, and though it may be imperfect in idealism and selflessness, it is appropriate to that particular phase in the individual's personal growth.

In sum, then, as men and their ideas vary or change, so, too, do their personal reasons for observing the *mitzvot.*

The rabbi cannot supply these motivations, for what may appeal to him is his personal affair, not some Olympian edict applying to everyone. A Jew is not free to decide whether or not a *mitzvah* itself is addressed to him; but every Jew is free, and indeed duty-bound, to meet the challenge of finding out *what* the observance of the *mitzvah* should mean to him as an individual. Don't ask someone else what *kashrut* should mean to *you*. Ask yourself, because no one can give you the answer. Others might provide *guidance,* but no one can supply your *answer.*

The next inference follows naturally: There is no such thing as a "wrong" answer to the question, "Why should *I* observe the *mitzvot*?" Any answer that inspires you to do the right thing is a "right" answer. To be sure, some motivations are nobler and less egocentric than others, and in this respect man should mature even as he matures in sensitivity and human compassion, in Torah learning and in warmth of spirit. But as long as the answer you have found fulfills its function—to induce you to do as you should—that answer is the "right" one you you.

Mitzvot
and Their Meaning

The *mitzvot* of the Torah are not all of one type; they are classed in three main categories, described by terms that indicate the dominant characteristics of each. Let us discuss the various types of *mitzvot* and then attempt to see their significance for the contemporary Jew.

1. *Mishpatim*, the "*mitzvot* of justice." These *mitzvot* are logical; their meaning is self-evident in that everyone accepts them as desirable and necessary. They are the laws that keep the wheels of society running smoothly and make it possible for men to live together without destroying one another. The *mishpatim* include the prohibitions against murder and theft, such laws as those pertaining to the establishment of courts, laws formulated and observed by society even without the teachings of the Torah.

2. *Edot*, literally "commemorative" *mitzvot*, or "Testimonials." It would probably not occur to us to devise the commandments that come into this category, but since these commandments are set forth in the Torah, any reasonable person with a sense of history will find them acceptable. Examples of *edot* are the festivals which commemorate important events in Jewish history. Passover, for instance, recalls the Exodus, and we are bidden to mark the occasion by ridding our homes of *chametz*, eating *matzah* and celebrating the *seder*. *Edot* have historical and didactic value which no one should find objectionable.

3. *Chukkim*, the "statutes," "fiats" or "decrees" of G-d. Our Sages refer to this category of *mitzvot* as the *mitzvot* that

are "ridiculed by the nations of the world (on the one hand) and by the *yetzer ha-ra* (evil impulse) of the Jew (on the other)." *Chukkim* have no rationale. When someone asks for an explanation of a *chok*, he is likely to receive a thoroughly unsatisfying shrug of the shoulder in reply. Examples of *chukkim* are the laws pertaining to the *parah adumah*, the "red heifer" whose ashes purify the defiled but defile the pure (Num. 19); *shatnez*, the prohibition against mixtures of wool and linen (Lev. 19:19); and, interestingly, the prohibition against the eating of pork (Lev. 11:7 and Deut. 14:8).

Of the three *mitzvah* categories, the *chukkim* alone are the ultimate test of faith. One need not be particularly devout to obey such *mishpatim* as the prohibition against murder and theft, and one may enjoy observing such *edot* as the Passover *seder* because of sentimental associations. Only the *chukkim* are observed for no other reason but that they are part of the Word of G-d.

In this connection, an interesting observation occurs to me. Many Jews of today wonder why their parents or grandparents were never able to explain to them in so many words why the Sabbath and *kashrut* should be observed. All that their elders were able to manage was an inarticulate stammer that "it says so in the Torah." On the face of it, this would seem to be a simple, naive way of dealing with the question. But it may be that, in fact, those "simple" elders were instinctively more enlightened than their sophisticated children. They sensed something about the origin of the *mitzvot* and about the capacities of the human mind as compared to the Divine Intellect. They observed all the *mitzvot*—not just the *chukkim,* but also the more "logical" *mishpatim* and *edot*—not because they understood them, but simply because these laws had come from G-d. They recognized in the *mitzvot* an element which no human mind can ever hope to fathom.

This may give us some insight into the pattern of the *mitzvot. Chukkim*—and, by extension, the other *mitzvot* as well—lie beyond the scope of our understanding. But we know that their observance creates a bond between man and his Creator, while their violation or neglect raises a barrier between man and G-d. The observances do make for personal satisfaction, social progress and cultural growth, but observing the *mitzvot* of the Torah is not contingent on these benefits.

The integration of the *mitzvot* brings the warmth and enthusiasm of the justice and testimonial laws into the *chukkim,* and the awareness of Divine origin inherent in the *chukkim* transforms the others into a religious experience.

Mitzvot:
Free Choice and Discipline

Mitzvot control so many aspects of human life from the most sublime thoughts and acts to the minutiae of daily existence. They present a network of obligations and prohibitions at every turn. What then becomes of human freedom, the freedom to choose? Man, we are constantly told, is unique. No two people are alike. How then can a single code apply to all equally without accommodation for differences between, say, an Einstein and a peasant? Moreover, the *mitzvot* themselves are repetitive actions. For instance, we recite the same prayers over and over again, several times every day, each day for a whole lifetime. What sense does this make?

Let me start with a personal observation. Today's society is probably less bound by religious strictures than any other in history. One might suppose that this lack of restrictions should have led to a flowering of individuality. How could it be otherwise if everyone has total freedom to choose his own life-style without being hampered by the narrow confines of religion?

And yet it appears that even when they have abandoned religion, men continue to conform. Conformity still seems to be the rule, for bankers and counter-culture alike. Freedom from religion does not automatically confer freedom to be oneself. I suggest that religion and personal freedom are not antithetical and that freedom is not identical with libertinism.

Compulsion may come from without, from family or society, but it may also be imposed from within, by the drives and desires that compel man to act to satisfy them.

A slave of Pharaoh is a slave, obviously; a slave of one's lusts is no less enslaved. Interestingly, Talmud states that slaves prefer *hefker,* lack of restraint, a state of license, implying that the slave had more freedom than the free man to indulge his desires.

Let us examine the idea of slavery imposed from within. If someone has a desire, why should he keep from satisfying that desire? Why should he ever deny himself? There is, after all, nothing to prevent him from doing so. (We are not talking here, of course, about the legal and social sanctions imposed by society, but only of what goes on within the person.) This person is *compelled* to gratify his lusts, and this compulsion is simply a synonym for slavery, the antithesis of freedom.

A free man is one who has options, who has the ability to choose from among alternatives. Note: I am saying "one who has the *ability,*" not only the *right,* to make his own choices. A color-blind man has the *right* to choose from among many colors, but his lack of ability precludes any meaningful choice. He is not, in any true sense, *free* to choose intelligently even between two neckties.

Torah offers man an option. His own desire tells him, "Do it!" but the Torah tells him, "Thou shalt not . . . " Thus man is rendered free, for he now has alternatives and the freedom to select between them. He can now reason about the alternatives and decide. It is not a matter of weighing advantages of one course over the other (if I steal that thing then I'll have it but I risk getting caught . . .), of prudence or utilitarian values, but a *moral* choice, based on considerations of right and wrong, even in cases where honesty is not the obviously best policy.

But, someone will protest, aren't you sugar-coating the bitter pill? Aren't you simply trying to answer away some burdensome restrictions? On the face of it, this point is well taken. But are mitzvos truly restrictions that hamper freedom of personal development? The artist is the traditional example of the free untrammelled spirit, the uninhibited Bohemian. But is the artist "free" in his art? Even he is subject to what, at first glance, appear to be restrictions: the size of his canvas, the properties of his marble, the tonal capacities of his violin. But is the painter working with a ten-foot canvas more "free" than the creator of a miniature? The restrictions imposed by the artist's materials do not inhibit his creative talents. Rather than denying his freedom, the framework within which he functions actually affords him the possibility and freedom to create.

Our society regards certain words, and the concepts they convey, with distaste. "Discipline" is a "dirty" word, evoking visions of a Prussian martinet, and the resulting distaste leads to disdain for any form of discipline when the fashionable goal is a blithe and free spirit. Again, back to the artist, that paradigm of the unfettered spirit. Is he really free of discipline?

A violinist must spend hours each day practicing on his instrument. One practice session missed and he instantly becomes aware that his performance is inadequate. What, actually, are the benefits—aside from improvement in his performance—that the artist derives from constant practice? Practice has trained his fingers to do, almost instinctively, what the music demands. On the concert stage he feels only the music. He is not distracted from the music by having to think where his fingers must go and what they are supposed to do. With his fingers working almost automatically, thanks to the discipline of regular practice, he is free do create and to express himself.

How delightful it would be if we could just create spontaneously, without preparation and forethought! Just get up on the stage in Carnegie Hall and play! You have so much feeling in you! Go ahead and express it. Alas, even an Isaac Stern and a Jascha Heifetz must practice.

Is true prayer easier to achieve than a perfect performance on the concert stage? I suggest that we cannot depend on spontaneity, on the spirit moving us whenever we choose to summon it. I recall being in a hospital with a family whose father was about to be wheeled into the operating room. The children kissed him and wished him well, suspecting they would never see him alive again. We all went to the synagogue to wait, and they wanted to pray. But they sat there mute, frustrated, unable to utter a word. To be sure, G-d hears the heart; He does not need verbal prayer. But these young men *wanted* to put their emotion into words, to express their pain, their fears, and their hopes. Here, it would seem, was an opportunity for spontaneous prayer, straight from the heart; here was the "concert stage" for loving children, and sadly, there was only an unrelieved silence for them.

We *daven* the same words every single day, several times a day, for years, for decades. Count how many times we have recited *Ashrei* by the time we are twenty, forty, eighty, They say even blintzes three times a day lose their flavor. How can we hope to find freshness and inspiration after reciting the same prayer thousands of times? But one day, suddenly, without warning, without any particular preparation, the words click! All of a sudden they make sense. You feel a surge—you are really *praying,* communicating with G-d. When will we be fortunate to have this experience? Of course we do not know, so we keep on *davening,* and when that moment comes we know it was worth all those efforts, that we could never have reached this moment otherwise.

(Another analogy from modern life: How many experiments must a scientist perform, how many attempts must an Edison make before he discovers what he seeks? Were any of his experiments, even those ending in blind alleys, really wasted efforts? Or were they a preparation of sorts for the discovery?)

Mitzvah performance is of the same order. The *mitzvah*-observing Jew trains himself to act in accordance with a Will superior to his own, to control his personal desires, to live by a moral code even when it may appear to be a burden. Then, without warning, he is catapulted onto the "concert stage." He is tested; he faces a moral problem ("Everyone is cheating—why shouldn't I" or "You have to pop pills or else you're left out"—you name it yourself). He will act properly, we hope. He will not have to fret about what to do, whose lead to follow, because he has already had long and diligent practice. He has lived by a moral code and he will continue to live by it. He is not afraid of being "different," nor will he be overwhelmed by temptation. No matter how complex the situation, how difficult the problem he faces, he will not have to meet the test without guidance.

(All this is not to say that *mitzvot* are just "rehearsals." Each *mitzvah* has its own intrinsic value,* a subject well worth exploring in detail. But here we are merely attempting to describe one particular beneficial effect of mitzvah living.)

Interestingly enough, the blandness and uniformity of our society is not characteristic of the Torah community. Within the framework of Torah there is wide latitude for individuality, for uniqueness, for personal expressions of thought and feeling. The same paints, brushes and canvas do not result in the same painting. The same *mitzvot* and observances do not yield the same personality.

Some people are intellectually inclined; among Jews this type is honored and not uncommon. In turn, even intellects vary, there are different fields of endeavor; there are analytic minds, retentive minds, profound, creative minds—the list has no end. All these minds are generously accommodated within Torah study itself. The "mystic," the passionate worshipper, the socially conscious, the extrovert, the introvert, the esthetic, and the practical, he who is isolated from all alien cultures and he who drinks deeply of all schools and ideas—all those have their place within the Torah community. They appear to have nothing in common, but they all live by the same Book. They all use the same instruments, yet each produces a melody uniquely his own.

Implicit in all this is the assumption that every Jew has the potential of being a Rembrandt of the soul.

---

*The essays "Speak English . . ." and "Tefillin Today" explore two *mitzvot*.

Mitzvot
in a Secular World

"How can I live as an observant Jew in a secular environment?" was the opening question at an Encounter session.

The test of individuality and personal integrity is the ability to maintain principles no matter what the environment in which one finds himself. Anything else is simply a reaction to forces. Perhaps one value of the Torah is that it gives the Jew the ability to rise above his environment, to control it and to influence it; in short, to dominate his environment instead of being its pawn.

This does not mean that the Torah would have the Jew become a maverick or a non-conformist; even oddballs take their cues from their environment—except that instead of submitting to it, their reaction is to rebel against it. Such individuals are not self-directed or guided by principles. Revolt for revolt's sake is a small virtue.

True, in some cases the environment in which one finds himself happens to be a desirable one. All well and good; if this is so, then you do not have to fight against your environment. However, you should accept it not because of consensus or consideration of personal popularity, or because "everybody's doing it," but because the standards of the society in which you live coincide with the principles you yourself cherish. If this is your attitude toward the environment, then you have not relinquished your individuality, your uniqueness, your integrity. (I might add here that the Rebbes frequently urged their *Chassidim* to create an environment of their own, even in the most unlikely places and societies.)

To be "different" is often the hardest decision to make. It is not so much the difficulty in "different" behavior, nor the financial or physical sacrifice that is an obstacle. The fact that you have elected to set yourself apart from the others, not to be part of the crowd, may arouse enmity from friends and objection from parents more than your behavior as such. Living a *mitzvah* life in a secular environment may mean, for instance, to decline certain invitations, or to wear some distinctive clothing (any getup may be acceptable on some campuses except modest dress . . .). No hardship is involved, but the discomfort is all too real. You have chosen to be on your own. Your resources are within yourself, and they guide you in deciding what your own values should be, and in living by these values. Your determination will be the decisive factor here.

However, observing *mitzvot* in a non-*mitzvah* environment may also present some practical (as distinct from intellectual or emotional) problems, such as keeping a job when you insist on observing the Sabbath and the holy days of the Jewish calendar, or wearing a *yarmulka* at your place of work. Fortunately, there is growing legal support for the Jew who wants to keep his job but refuses to compromise his religious principles. In every situation the human factor must be handled in its own terms without magic, all-purpose formulas. It should be encouraging to note that the phenomenon of a thoroughly observant Jew successful in his chosen career is no longer an oddity. This does not mean that it's roses all the way, but it *is* being done.

Good, Evil
and the Intellect

One of the reasons for the opposition which *Chassidus* encountered in its early days was the fear that the new movement might be under the influence of certain destructive tendencies that were rife in Judaism at the time. One of these trends was a particularly reprehensible perversion of the *Kabbalah* by certain adherents of the pseudo-Messiah Jacob Frank, who indulged in orgies with the explanation that they were bringing about redemption through impurity; the coming of the Messiah, they said, could be hastened if the entire world were hopelessly under the spell of evil. Eventually the "Frankists" cited this argument as an excuse for every moral foulness; they explained it in lofty, idealistic terms as spiritually and self-sacrifice rather than as gross hedonism. It seems plausible that the evils of "Frankism" were the problem to which the Alter Rebbe, the founder of *Chabad Chassidus,* addressed himself in *Likutei Torah* (Balak 69 and Song of Songs 31 b and c).

Chabad philosophy has a definite view on the place of intellect in the structure and fulfillment of the human soul. The Rebbe postulates two broad areas of "soul powers"— the intellectual and the emotive. The soul, which, of course, is non-corporeal, manifests itself on the highest plane through its intellectual faculties, particularly in *chochmah* (the flash of insight), and then in descending order through *binah* (comprehension and development) and finally to its conclusion in *daat* ("knowledge"). At this point emotion comes into play, for intellect engenders appropriate feelings such as love or fear, attraction or withdrawal, and so forth. For our present purposes it is sufficient to state the critical point: emotions are not necessarily capricious; they can be generated, controlled or even extirpated by force of the intellect. The proposition that mind has dominion over the heart is a basic tenet of *Chabad* philosophy.

The intellect rules supreme. The Alter Rebbe's high regard for intellect is evident from the fact that he named his school of *Chassidus* "*Chabad*" (an acronym for *chochmah, binah,* and *daat*). But he does not deify the mind. To him the mind is still only one power of the soul, not some ultimate. Intellect may be the dominant one among man's faculties, it can determine the quality of the person and of his life, but it is not yet the summit. There are areas where intellect is inoperative, for example in the supradimensional, or in matters beyond man's experience (pure spirit, eschatology, etc.). Thus, faith is characterized as transcending the mind; it is valid where intellect is irrelevant. But these particular limitations on intellect are not important for our present purposes.

In our own day we face a problem concerning intellect which does not seem to have troubled earlier generations, the capacity of the mind to formulate moral definitions. Philosophers have wrestled with these definitions since antiquity, confident that the answer was within reach. Only in the relatively recent past has it been recognized that the tools of intellect are not relevant to moral concepts such as right and wrong, good and evil, in short—morality. Here we recognize a critical limitation on the competence of the mind, a recognition which eluded man until about the present century. The Alter Rebbe, with all his reverence for intellect, clearly delineates its shortcomings in the moral sphere.

The Biblical term "tree of the knowledge of good and evil" (Gen. 2:17) describes the very nature of knowledge. Knowledge is a mixture of good and evil; it is not totally in the one camp or in the other. The direction which the mind can take, the imperatives dictated by the intellect, may be either good or evil; one choice is not more "rational" than the other. The mind may point in one direction, but it may just as validly point in the other. The mind is therefore quite useless when it comes to defining what is good or to offering guidance to man in his moral dilemmas.

The soul, of which the mind is a power, derives from a source with a potential for both good and evil. When the mind devotes itself to the contemplation of the Divine, when it rationally acknowledges man's total dependence on G-d, Who grants or witholds life itself, then the direction which the mind will indicate, the emotions which it will arouse, and the actions it will effect and control will be "good." The person will then love G-d, cleave to Him, and be eager to do His will. On the other hand, if the mind is otherwise occupied, then the blandishments of self-indulgence, the immediate and compelling desire for gratification may enlist the mind's aid in making them intellectually "respectable," indeed imperative and "good." Hence, good and evil are irrelevant concepts on the plane of intellect. Good and evil are commingled on the plane of knowledge. Before a choice can be made, it is necessary to arrive at a definition of "good" and "evil," but such a definition is not a function of intellect.

Knowledge, the Rebbe declares, is incapable of totally repelling evil, or of defining evil, since knowledge itself is in need of clarification, of a line of demarcation between good and evil in its own sphere. Even as the person has the capacity for both good and evil, so, too, knowledge harbors antagonistic forces within itself.

R. Shneur Zalman dedicates his primary work, the *Tanya*, to the *benoni*, the man who has arrived at the "intermediate" stage between good and evil, whose every thought, word and deed are dedicated, but whose potential for evil is undiluted and who must therefore struggle unceasingly to contain that potential. According to the Talmud (*Berachot* 61b), the Rebbe states, the *benoni* is "judged" by both the good and evil within himself. The evil is untouched, unsubdued, unconverted, ever ready to tempt the *benoni* away from the Divine and toward evil. Mind, alas, is helpless in overcoming evil, for the mind itself contains evil.

For a man to undertake the purification of evil is indeed a noble venture, but before one can purify anything else, one must be pure oneself. "Adorn yourself and then adorn others," the Talmud (*Sanhedrin* 18a) wryly counsels. The Rebbe takes a dim view of those who boldly embark on the purification of evil. He does not, of course, denigrate the task itself, but he questions the qualifications of those who volunteer for it. In Chapter 28 of *Tanya* he derides the "idiots" who seek to "elevate" alien thoughts that occur during worship or Torah study, for "how can (a man) elevate (anything) when he himself is bound below?"

But aware though we are of the limits of intellect, are we to be frustrated in coping with the unavoidable task of making moral choices, of formulating definitions of "good" and "evil"? Apparently, if we are concerned only with the manifest powers of the soul, such as mind and emotion, we will arrive at an impasse. But man has more resources than these.

It may be said that man and G-d are analogous. On the one hand, man was made "in His image"; on the other hand, man declares that *"from my flesh* I perceive G-d." G-d permeates Creation; He reveals Himself in all His works; He "fills all the worlds." Immanent G-d may be revealed more in some circumstance, or to one individual, and less in another situation or to a less sensitive person. At the same time, G-d is transcendent: He is removed from Creation; He "encompasses" Creation, in contrast to "permeating" Creation, and before Him there is no such thing as "high" or "low." (The term for this, *sovev,* indicates a circle that has no higher or lower.) In the presence of the Transcendent, there can only be nullity. These two categories—immanence and transcedence—exist also in human terms, with appropriate adaptations, of course.

Man possesses both an animal soul and a Divine soul.
The animal soul is directed to worldly pursuits and com-
prises both good and evil. The Divine strives only after G-d
and is null, self-less, in His presence. Both souls have intellectual and emotive powers. Immanence is related to the
animal soul, and transcendence to the Divine soul. The
mind of the earthly, animal soul generates feelings of attraction to worldly pleasures, while the intellect of the
Divine soul creates love and awe of G-d. It is obvious that
these two disparate strivings come into conflict with one
another. The *daat elyon,* the "superior intelligence" of the
Divine soul, summons forth the state of nullification (*bitul*),
eliciting the very essence of the soul, overwhelming the
person's awareness of self, making him conscious only of
the transcendent and nullifying the emotions generated by
the *daat tachton,* the "inferior intellect" of the animal soul.

Here we have one function of prayer as *Chabad* conceives
it. One who experiences intense concentration, deep contemplation of G-d's unity and uniqueness as he recites the
Sh'ma, will feel that he, too, is null before G-d, an instrument of G-d free of all other considerations. Then the
animal soul is cleansed of its material dross and evil becomes alien to it; the "transformation" is taking place.

This "transformation" is not an intellectual exercise, an
attempt to master complex subject matter, as Torah study
would be. Here the critical issue is the summoning of the
capacity of *bitul,* of self-nullification, from within the recesses of the soul, to engage an element of soul which transcends the intellect and touches closer to the essence of soul
itself. Intellectual meditation on the grandeur of G-d, for
instance, may be quite effective in arousing love and reverence for G-d, because both mind and heart are then effectively involved, but the effects of such meditation will not
be enduring because the selfhood of the individual, of the
animal soul, remains unchanged; no *bitul* has taken place.
Bitul alone can keep man from subsequently losing the
inspiration he experienced during worship.

Intellect cannot challenge *bitul,* or the conclusions drawn from it. Intellect cannot persuade man (as it could in the absence of *bitul*) that indulgence is "good," because when *bitul* is present, the intellect's capacity for evil, its aloofness from moral definitions, is eliminated; intellect itself then leads only to the concluion that the Divine alone is "good."

There is yet another definition for *bitul* as such. The soul is known by several designations, each referring to a level or aspect dominant in a given situation. *Nefesh* implies action; *ruach,* emotion; and *neshama,* intellect. *Chaya-Yechida* is the essence of soul. *Yechida*—unique, united, indivisible, joined completely with its Creator, utterly self-effacing, far beyond what intellect might dictate. The epithet "stiffnecked people" is not derogatory but an accolade for Israel, because it indicates that Israel's devotion to G-d transcends rationality, that the people of Israel are prepared at all times to make the ultimate sacrifice, martyrdom, that survival for the sake of mere self-preservation is meaningless to them. *Bitul*—stiff-neckedness, and *yechida*—indivisibility, are parallels.

When *yechida* is manifest, man rises above the intellectual choice we have noted, above the ambivalence inherent in the mind. The very potential for evil is destroyed. *Yichud,* "unity" effected by man, is the coalescing of the animal and Divine souls, the "superior" and "inferior" intelligences, the transcendent and the immanent. This state is brought about by prayer, elevating the lower to the higher, so that the original base characteristics are lost and the qualities of the superior acquired. The transcendent then becomes immanent, and the intellect repudiates evil.

Ahavas Yisrael—
"Love Your Fellow As Yourself"

In assessing the creative contribution of *Chassidus,* it is necessary to remember the old *Chassidic* adage: *Chassidus* did not add a 614th *mitzvah* to the original 613, nor did it annul any of the 613 *mitzvot.* Rather, *Chassidus* gave new vitality to the *mitzvot.* Whatever may seem to be novel in *Chassidic* thought or practice is ultimately rooted in Torah tradition and based on Torah precedent that may have been only implicit previously, or, for some reason, had fallen into neglect. *Chassidus* simply re-emphasized what already existed before, infusing it with new spirit, giving it a centrality it did not enjoy.

The contribution of *Chassidus* does not consist in innovations but in its manner of presenting classic Jewish values in terms of contemporary need. When *Chassidus* first emerged on the Jewish scene it reawakened a virtue which had long lain dormant and which subsequently became a part of active Judaism for all the generations that followed. That dormant *mitzvah* is *ahavas Yisrael,* the love for all one's fellow Jews, which proclaims the sanctity of even the least of souls. the eternal, irrevocable bond between Israel and G-d, and between one Jew and all other Jews, regardless of personal merit or social station. It was resuscitated, as it were, by the Baal Shem T´v, founder of Chassidus.

A brief historical note is in order here. In the Baal Shem's day, in the Eastern Europe of the early half of the 18th century, the Jewish people was cleft in two; the scholar was separated from the ordinary Jew by a barrier that appeared all but insurmountable. To be sure, the scholar class was not hereditary or sacerdotal, but one founded on personal merit based on ability and diligent study. Anyone, regardless of economic position or rabbinic family background, could become a Torah scholar, if he had the mental capacity and was willing to apply himself to his studies. In this respect, the "merit system" of Torah scholarship was supremely democratic and egalitarian. Nevertheless, it had the effect of placing the scholar on a level higher than that of the ordinary, untutored Jew.

The barrier between scholar and untutored effectively prevented communication between the two—and the mutual benefits that would have inevitably resulted from such ties. All too often the scholar looked down upon the simple folk with such contempt that he even denied them ordinary courtesies in public worship at the synagogue. At the same time, the untutored were mercilessly chastised by the itinerant preachers (*maggidim*) of the period, who denounced even their slightest shortcomings in sharp language, depicting in vivid detail the hellish torments awaiting the souls of these incorrigible sinners.

Thus the untutored were not only depressed by what they perceived to be their spiritual shortcomings but were even denied the hope of a better afterlife. Their economic condition was equally dismal. The devastating Cossack pogroms of 1648–49 had left the Jews of Eastern Europe destitute, hopeless and leaderless. The shattered community was in need of drastic action, imaginative and devoted leadership. These the *Chassidic* movement provided in the form of practical measures, a new ideology and unusual leaders. Notably, as we have said before, the *Chassidic* movement revived the concept of *ahavas Yisrael.* At the time this was a startling idea, but it was hardly revolutionary in substance.

We might say that in his emphasis on *ahavas Yisrael,* the Baal Shem Tov worked in two directions simultaneously. Stirred by his own intense love for his fellow Jews, he devoted his life to their rehabilitation, spiritual as well as material. At the same time, he endeavored to arouse similar feelings also in other Jews as part of his campaign to rejuvenate the Jewish community.

For years the Baal Shem Tov traveled through Jewish villages, gathering untutored men, women and children, and telling them tales to introduce them to Torah and Jewish living in terms that they could understand. Thus, he used a parable to explain the importance of *ahavas Yisrael* by depicting the greatness of G-d's own love for the Jewish people. A great scholar was immersed in his studies when he was interrupted by his little son's childish prattle. The sage put aside his tomes to play with his child. "Only his own child could make this sage interrupt his studies," the Baal Shem explained. "In the same manner, G-d interrupts His 'affairs' to listen to the prayers of His children. And why does he cherish their prayers? Listen and I will tell you why. When G-d told the angels at the time of Creation that He was going to create man, the angels asked Him, 'What is man that you should take note of him? Why do you need a being such as man?'

"Well, when a Jew wakes up early in the morning, rushes off to *shul* to *daven* with the early *minyan,* then spends all day earning his meager livelihood, and still drops everything to *daven mincha* in shul, and between *mincha* and *ma'ariv* he listens to some *Ain Ya'akov,* and when he comes home and repeats the lesson to his wife and children . . . The G-d summons His angels and proudly points to that man, whom He created. 'You angels do not have to make a living. You have no wives and children to feed. You have neither business worries nor heavy taxes. But this man *does* have all these cares and obligations, and yet, with all the burdens of exile and taxes, see how he lives—all because I commanded him to do it, because all this is part of My Torah."

G-d Himself is proud of this man. Is man, then, not deserving that other people should also love him? Incidentally, *ahavas Yisrael* is now an integral part of the Jewish scale of values, no less than filial devotion, worship and the study of Torah.

The Baal Shem Tov's disciple and successor, Reb Dov Ber, the Maggid of Mezrich, described his mentor's *ahavas Yisrael* as "beyond description." Almost wistfully, he remarked, "If only we could kiss the Torah with the same love that the Baal Shem Tov embraced the small children he brought to *heder* when he was a *behelfer,* a teacher's assistant." He would often quote his master's statements on *ahavas Yisrael.* One of these, in fact, was one of the first which the Alter Rebbe heard in Mezrich. "Love of Israel is love of G-d. 'You are children of the L-rd your G-d' (Deut. 14:1). He who loves the Father also loves the children."

The Baal Shem Tov stressed the urgency of *ahavas Yisrael* in the strongest terms. Once, at a large public assembly in the city of Brody, he said:

> "G-d sends a soul down into this world,
> To live for seventy or eighty years;
> The ultimate purpose of his mission is
> To do someone a favor;
> A material favor in general;
> A spiritual favor in particular."

His successors, particularly the *Chabad* Rebbes, quoted these words over and over again, not as a theoretical abstraction, but as a guide for everyday life.

This wonderful trait of *ahavas Yisrael* has been expressed over the generations in countless priceless ways: in help given the poor while preserving the dignity of the recipients, in sharing the anguish of widows and orphans by comforting them and aiding them in their distress.

Before long, *Chassidus* had spread to encompass the great bulk of East European Jewry. Wherever it gained a foothold, it brought with it a reactivated *ahavas Yisrael* as a revived, integral aspect of Jewish living.

* * * * * *

R. Menachem Mendel, the third Rebbe of Lubavitch, wrote a lengthy discourse on the subject of Ahavas Yisrael. *The following translation may serve as a text:*

In two consecutive verses (Lev. 19:17 and 18), the Torah speaks out against hatred: "Do not hate your brother in your heart . . . You shall not take vengeance, nor bear any grudge against your people; you shall love your fellow as yourself."

Hillel's explanation to the proselyte who wanted to learn everything about Judaism while standing on one leg is familiar. "Whatever is hateful to you, do not do to your fellow man. That is the entire Torah. The rest is interpretation. Now go and study."

How could Hillel have described this one commandment as comprising the entire Torah? Obviously, it is one of the *mitzvot* governing relations of man and man. But what connection does it have with the *mitzvot* pertaining to man's relations with G-d? As early an authority as the *Ari,** who was active long before the emergence of *Chassidus,* taught that before beginning one's prayers, one should recite the formal affirmation of the *mitzvah* of *ahavas Yisrael,* since it is an indispensable beginning of the worship of G-d. "I assume the positive *mitzvah* of "You shall love your fellow as yourself." (This affirmation was incorporated into the *Chabad* prayer book.)

The *Ari* states that the community of Israel may be compared to one single body, the body comprising numerous individual organs. (In Kabbalistic terms, the community of Israel is compared to the soul of Adam, since Adam comprised all souls, all humanity issuing from him.) Each individual within that body corresponds to one of the body's organs. This is the reason why each individual Jew is held accountable for the failings of all others. R. Hayim Vital, the *Ari*'s greatest disciple, noted that his master regularly recited the full *Viddui* (Confession of Sins), an expression of this responsibility.

---

*Rabbi Issac Luria (1534—72), the famous Kabbalist of Safed.

According to the Kabbalist interpretation, Adam incorporated all the souls of Israel, with some corres-
ponding to the "head," others to the "arm," and so
forth. This unitary source of individual souls, in turn, has
a parallel on an even higher plane. The intellectual and
emotional powers of the soul roughly parallel the
sephirot or "attributes" of G-d Himself. Each of these
attributes could occur in an isolated form, uninfluenced
by any of the others. Thus the attribute of chessed
(kindness) would then be untempered by its antithesis,
gevurah (sternness). On the other hand, the attributes
could commingle and be modified by one another.
Thus, sternness would put restraints on kindness, while
kindness would temper sternness. This mutual interac-
tion takes place by design of a still higher influence,
which is superior to them all: the Infinite. The Infinite
includes within itself all these lower attributes and indeed, all forms of existence. "For they all derive from
You" (I Chron. 29:14). Thus, before they ever attained
their individuality, all the attributes already existed, albeit in a submerged state, where there are no differences and distinctions. For this reason, even after
attaining the state of individual entities, they are still
capable of resubmerging their differences and re-
uniting. This, too, occurs under the influence of the
Infinite.

Let us return to the comparison of the Jewish community with the body of a man. The body is composed
of many organs; some of these have higher functions,
or are more sensitive, than others. Thus, the head contains the "higher" faculties; the foot, the power of
locomotion. The fingernails, by contrast, are not even
sensitive to pain. But notwithstanding these wide variations, none of these organs are independent of the
others. For example, infection of one organ—or treat-
ment of one organ—affects others. This interdependence derives from their common source, the life force,
which is harbored in the brain and diffused from there

throughout the body. The brain is sensitive to pain in a distant, less "vital" organ.

The souls, or as they were originally termed, the "organs" of Adam, were completely united in their common source, the Divine attribute of *chochmah* (wisdom), which is united with Him. G-d refers to Israel as "My son, my first-born" (Exodus 4:22). The soul is derived from G-d much as the child originates from his father, and in their source, as already noted, there is fusion of souls.

Still, notwithstanding their indivisible source, the souls do separate into innumerable individual entities, each in its own body, just as each human body is composed of individual organs. However, the "separateness" of the individual is more superficial than actual. True, each individual is physically separate from all others, but the soul is not divided. The analogy of the human body will serve us well here. No bodily organ can remain completely unaffected by trouble in any of the others. Basically, they form one united whole. So, too, the souls of Israel are not truly separate from one another but affect each other because they are part of one inseparable entity.

We can now understand why the saintly *Ari* should have felt it necessary to recite the full *Viddui* for sins possibly committed by other persons. The soul of the sinner was much inferior to that of the *Ari*, but the *Ari* felt the "pain" of each one, because his soul was linked with them all. The soul of the *Ari*, with the souls of all the others, was included within the same source, the "wisdom" of the Father, Who is sensitive to the pain of even the least among the "organs."

This sheds new light on the *mitzvah* of *ahavas Yisrael*. We now see that it is based on the fact that all souls are intermingled even as all the organs of the body are joined. In paraphrase, each individual contains within himself the other person as well. Conversely, that individual in turn is part of the other.

Hence, the commandment, "You shall love your neighbor *as yourself.*"

As we prepare to recite our prayers, the *Ari* declares, we reaffirm our acceptance of this *mitzvah.* As he recites the *Sh'ma,* particularly the word *echad,* the final word of the first verse ("Hear, O Israel, the L-rd our G-d *is One*"), the worshipper attains a state of complete devotion. However, he cannot attain this level unless his soul is "complete" in its composition; that is, unless his own soul is fully united with all other souls. Only in this state of unity can the worshipper ascend before G-d, the source of all souls. Only when united with other souls can the individual soul rise to the source from which it came.

When an individual carries a grudge in his heart against his fellow, he has "amputated" part of himself, a part of his own soul which is represented in that of the other, since the other is part of himself. In his hatred he has rejected what is actually a part of himself. Inevitably, this "amputation" produces a defect in his own soul, and he becomes a spiritual cripple. This handicap prevents him from ascending before G-d in worship, for it is written in Leviticus 21:17 that "whoever has a defect shall not approach . . . "

* * * * * *

The Maggid of Mezrich asks a question fundamental to *Chassidic* doctrine. A man can compel himself to perform a physical act. Thus, he can force his hand to give charity even though his heart is not in it. He may compel his mind to study or to meditate even though he may have no real desire to do so, and he does it only because he considers it the proper or necessary thing to do. But how can one force himself to love, or to fear, or to refrain from hatred on command? If one feels love within his heart, then he has that feeling, but if he does not, what good could a commandment do?

The Maggid posed this question with regard to the

commandment, "you shall love the L-rd your G-d with all your heart . . . " (Deut. 6:5), but of course it applies equally to the commandment of "love your fellow." The Alter Rebbe explains that the commandment to love our G-d was put after, and not before, verse 4, "Hear, O Israel, the L-rd our G-d is One," to indicate that when one truly comprehends and meditates deeply on *Sh'ma,* one will inevitably come to love G-d. The *mitzvah* to love G-d, in effect, is the *mitzvah* to meditate, and thus to create love where it might not exist otherwise. The word *ve'ahavta,* you shall love, may properly be translated as, you *will* love, an assurance rather than a command.

This brings us to another basic *Chabad* doctrine—the relationship between intellect and emotion. *Chabad* asserts that man is capable of controlling every aspect of his life. Just as he can control his actions, so, too, he can control his thoughts and his emotions. Thoughts and feelings are no more products of chance than are deeds.

The concept noted above in the essay "What is Chassidus," *moach shalit al ha-lev,* the mind has dominion over the heart, is rooted in the Torah, but the Alter Rebbe expounds it as the basis for a system of serving G-d. Man may relinquish his mastery over his emotions, and permit himself to become their pawn, but that is a decision on his part, not something which he "cannot help" because it is "part of his nature." He may not be able to control his heartbeat, but he can control his heart's feelings if he wills it. The key is his intellect. Appropriate meditation on G-d's greatness will lead man to feelings of awe and reverence; thoughts of G-d's kindness will inspire him with sentiments of love and gratitude.

The verb *ve'ahavta,* "you shall love," is used to introduce both the *mitzvah* of loving G-d (Deut. 6:5) and that of loving one's fellow men (Lev. 19:18). The key to generating both kinds of love is the same—the use of the mind, and development of the intellect in such a manner that the heart will reflect the conclusions of the mind, that thought and feeling will be harmonious, both of them having been developed by man as a free being. Love of another is not necessarily spontaneous. Some people are eminently un-lovable. Nevertheless, they, too, are re'acha, "your fellow," flesh of your flesh, or, better, soul of your soul.

Hillel said to the prospective convert to Judaism, "Whatever is hateful to you, do not do to your fellow man. That is the entire Torah. The rest is interpretation. Now go and study." (Parenthetically the last sentence frequently gets lost in the shuffle of quotation.) How could Hillel say that all the other commandments in the Torah are "commentary" on the one *mitzvah* of not doing to others what one would not like to have done to oneself.* Obviously, *mitzvot* involving relationships between human beings can be classed as "commentary" to this commandment. For instance, we do not want to be robbed ourselves, so we also should not rob others. But can *mitzvot* pertaining to relationships between man and G-d be called "commentaries" to *mitzvot* governing interhuman relationships? How do the *mitzvot* of, say, putting on *tefillin* every morning or eating *matzot* on Passover, offer comment on "love your neighbor"?

The explanation lies in the attitude toward body and soul and the relationship between the two. In Chapter 32 of the *Tanya*, the Rebbe declares: "There can be no genuine feelings of love and brotherliness among those who stress the body and regard their souls as secondary. They can attain no more than a love that is dependent on some (external) factor." The man-G-d relationship requires an acceptance of the soul and its values. Without this acceptance of the soul, the *Tzemach Tzedek* (R. Menahem Mendel, grandson of the Alter Rebbe) explains, the physical body is at least dominant if it is not the totality of man, and in that case, what deep bond can there exist between man and his neighbor? Except, perhaps, for utilitarian considerations ("I'll stop when I get the red light, and I hope you'll stop when you do"), man has no identification with another, no reason to sacrifice his welfare or even his personal comfort

*Rabbi Akiva's words are almost a paraphrase. "Love your neighbor as yourself—this is the great general principle of the Torah."

for another, for he is a separate entity, with no link to his fellow man. So the man-to-man *mitzvot* are contingent on accepting the soul.

The common soul is the only bond joining men, for physically they are separate, unconnected. The soul, then, is the basis for man-to-man *mitzvot,* just as it is the basis for man-to-G-d *mitzvot.*

Of course, there are many "non-religious" individuals who are highly moral and ethical. But they did not create their own ethical codes; they inherited them. There is a moral and cultural reservoir, as it were, of which some partake even though they deny the wellspring of that reservoir. (See the essay, "Three Stages.") The point here is that the ultimate reason for the stress placed on the *mitzvah* of loving one's neighbor is not mere sentimentality. Mathematicians, I understand, can "create" entire universes with laws different from our own, and so it is not surprising that moralists can articulate ever more noble ethical declarations. The Torah presents us with a consistent system, which places man and his fellow into a definite context, gives meaning to life and to human relationships, and is powerful enough to inspire man to place something other than himself at the center of his universe. The "non-religious" are not independent of religion.

In *ahavas Yisrael* we have a core principle presented as the basis for *all mitzvot,* in essence eliminating categories such as "man-man relationships" and "man-G-d relationships" except for purposes of convenience. Neither category of *mitzvah* can exist without the other, nor, in fact, is either truly distinct from the other. One relationship with G-d is dependent on one's love for his fellow men. When man's love for another is determined by "external factors," such as prudence or convenience or mutual safety, then when these factors fall away, the two men must clash. An interpersonal relationship can survive external changes only if it is an encounter of soul with soul.

But "soul" is a tenuous concept, impalpable and invisible, not only to the naked eye. Human encounters do involve "external factors" that conceal the soul. Let us review a *Chabad* concept already noted in the essay, "Chassidic Attitudes to Other Jews." This should lead us to an understanding of soul.

Chabad differentiates between *etzem* (essence) and *hispashtus* (extension). The former is irreducible, concealed, incorruptible, and constant. The second is obvious, manifest, and in a perpetual state of flux. When speaking of a "thing" of any kind, we must remember to distinguish between its *etzem* and *hispashtus*; if we do not do so, we may become confused, or assume a conflict where none exists.

For example, in discussing G-d, the authors of classic Rabbinical literature describe Him in different terms, and often seem to disagree with each other, sharply at times. Recognizing the distinction between *etzem* and *hispashtus* largely eliminates what appear to be conflicts. The sages who seem to disagree are simply describing different aspects of *hispashtus,* the "externals" of G-d, and each author is correct.

When we speak of G-d's *hispashtus,* we might understand it better by studying man. Man, being created in the image of G-d, gives us insight into Him, and whatever we can perceive of G-d's "nature" will give us insight into ourselves.

Let us examine *etzem* and *hispashtus* in man. *Chassidus* frequently refers to the three "garments" of the soul— thought, speech and deed. It is primarily on the basis of these three that we relate and respond to others. We are attracted, or repelled, by the thoughts, words and acts of the other.

Man's thoughts, however, are not identical with his self. *Chassidus* holds that intellect and thought are virtually identical with the *etzem,* because thought is directed inward; no other person is aware of what you are thinking at any given moment. Also, thought is constant—appearances to the contrary nonwithstanding, no mind is ever truly blank. The activity of thought would seem to be identical with that of the soul, for both activities go on unceasingly. However, soul is *not* mind. The individual *has* thoughts, but he is not synonymous with thoughts. Thoughts change. What was not understood yesterday is clear today; what was accepted yesterday is challenged today. Man's intellect grows. "Man" and "intellect," "man" and "thought" are not synonyms.

Speech is further removed from man than is thought. While thought is self-contained and can flourish in isolation, speech is a form of communication to the outside and presupposes the existence of another individual. And since, as *Koheles* puts it (Chapter 3:7), there is a "time to keep silent and a time to speak," speech is not constant but intermittent. Actions, of coure, are quite distinct from the person. Take the table before you. Whoever made this table may be long dead, but this does not affect the existence of the table, which is the product of his actions. Thought, speech, and action, then, the manifestations of soul, are "externals"; nevertheless, we predicate our relationships on them.

Here *Chassidus* presents us with an abstraction that has tremendous possibilities for practical application. Do not be misled by *hispashtus,* the "externals," we are told. Rather, look to *etzem,* the incorruptible core, or, to put it more precisely, the soul. We may approve or disapprove of the soul's "garments," but we must not confuse them with the person himself. We may detest his ideas, his language, or his actions; if so, let us teach him something better, but let us not look down upon him. His *etzem* is soul, and soul in turn is nothing less than a spark of G-d. Therefore, if you reject an individual you reject G-d, and that cannot be.

The challenge is twofold; it goes out to both the "observer" and the "subject." The observer is challenged to penetrate the subject's shell, the husk and the chaff—the *hispashtus*—which are not the real person, and call forth the pristine soul, the spark of G-d within man. The subject, in turn, is challenged to bring his externals, the "garments" in which his soul is clothed, into harmony with his soul, to eliminate any contradiction that may exist between the essence of his soul and his way of life. That is what Torah is all about.

How can one acquire the quality of *ahavas Yisrael*? If we recognize that the reality of the individual is not what we see, but what he is, and if we address ourselves to the *neshama,* the inner core, rather than to the outer shell, we will obtain a response. It is not enough for one who seeks to acquire *ahavas Yisrael* to speak with his mouth alone. It is only when soul calls that soul answers.

Avodah

In *Chabad* terminology familiar terms acquire new meanings which, though inherent in the term *per se,* are not commonly associated with it. In many instances it is more a matter of new emphasis than of new meaning, but this makes *Chabad's* contribution no less valid.

Let us examine the term *avodah,* which is generally rendered as "worship" or "service." The Talmudic expression *avodah shebalev,* "service of the heart." refers to prayer. The famed triad in the Ethics of the Fathers, the three pillars on which Creation stands,* includes *avodah.* Translations of the Ethics usually render *avodah* as "Divine Service," or, more specifically, the "service at the Sanctuary." Of course the *Chabad* interpretation does not intend to supersede these two definitions; nevertheless, it has directed attention to a connotation that presents *avodah* in an unusual light.

The Alter Rebbe conceived of *avodah* in terms of its literal, straightforward meaning: "work" or "labor." To him, the value of worship (or the more inclusive term, "service," for besides the "service of the heart" there is "service of the intellect" through study, and there are others who serve G-d with "body"—by acts of kindness, for example, and those who serve Him with their possessions—by giving charity) depended on the "labor" or "effort" expended by the individual in the act. While the Rebbe had high regard for mental and spiritual endow-

---

*Upon three things the world is based: upon *Torah, avodah,* and *gemilut chasadim"* (1:2).

ment, he was far more impressed with achievement born of constant striving. In this view, then, *avodah* exists quite apart from such other values as scholarship and piety, qualities which may well be the effects of natural gifts with no personal effort involved.

The *Tanya*, the basic Chabad work the Alter Rebbe wrote, is primarily concerned with the *benoni*, the individual who is in the "intermediate" stage between the wicked and the saintly, rather than with the *tzaddik*, the saint who has already succeeded in overcoming the evil within himself. The *benoni* still holds within himself the evil capacity for both good and evil; he represents the battleground between these two forces. His virtue is that he never permits evil to gain control over him and that he never actually commits a sin; however, he has the potential for sin. The *tzaddik*, by contrast, has already overcome the evil within him, his battle is over. The *Tanya* refers to the *tzaddik* as an *eved*, a "servant" of G-d. The noun "servant" implies that he has already achieved a permanent status vis-a-vis the Creator. The *benoni* may or may not be classed as an *oved*, one who is "serving" G-d. (Note the difference between being a "servant" and merely "serving.") Whether or not a *benoni* is indeed *oved* ("serving") depends on the effort he must expend in the struggle against the evil within him. Conceivably, the Rebbe points out, a *benoni* may be an introvert, a born student indifferent to the desires of the flesh. This student may indeed devote himself unreservedly to Torah study and to the meticulous observance of the *mitzvot*, and never fall prey to sin. But whatever his virtues, the Rebbe asserts, they are not the fruits of his labors; they are natural outgrowths of his innate proclivities, not the products of deliberate effort, of *avodah*.

In this connection, the Rebbe cites a Biblical verse: "You will perceive the difference between the saintly and the wicked, between him who serves G-d and him who does not serve Him" (Malachi 3:18). The Talmud explains that, as a matter of fact, the one who "does not serve Him" is not "wicked," at least not in this particular context. It interprets the latter part of the verse as comparing not the saint and the sinner, but two "good" people, one of whom expends deliberate effort in the service of G-d, while the other serves G-d without unduly exerting himself. Saintliness and "service" are two distinct concepts. Virtue may come with ease, while effort may well yield only undistinguished gains. But the *benoni* who attains and maintains his state without particular effort, is denied the encomium of *oved*. In the Rebbe's view, *avodah* is no less important than study, worship and observance. It is a new dimension in man's service of G-d.

The Rebbe extends the concept one step further, citing the Talmudic analogy (*Chagiga* 96) of a wagon driver who charges a reasonable fare for a long but accustomed route but takes double the amount when he has to go beyond the distance to which he is accustomed, even though the extra distance is small. He charges a disproportionately high amount for the extra distance because it is more than his usual route. Even one who is not a natural student, the Rebbe says, but has forced himself to study assiduously (when he exerts this effort, he becomes an *oved*) can become so completely accustomed to studying that it becomes "natural" for him, a routine journey which no longer requires any special effort on his part. When he reaches the stage where study becomes second nature to him, he ceases to be an *oved*. If he is to be an *oved* again, he must put forth a new effort beyond the pursuits which have become routine to him, he must break into new territory. This holds good not only for study. Prayer and charity may also become routine, and only by extending their horizons can one bring them back into the realm of true *avodah*.

The standard here is a subjective one, and depends entirely on the individual concerned. In the case of the *benoni*, "perfect *avodah*" may consist in arousing within himself that impelling love of G-d which can overcome the forces of habit. Perhaps his arousal of the latent love of G-d within him may enable him to do no more than merely discipline his evil impulse. But whatever the result of the effort, it may properly be called *avodah*. On the other hand, if he attains love of G-d without any struggle, then this love *per se,* no matter how great, cannot be described as *avodah*.

The Rebbe urges each individual to evaluate himself dispassionately to determine whether his service to G-d is as intense as it might be, in fervent worship and in resolute battle with his body and his "animal soul." Whether the person can barely control his base lusts, or whether his spiritual endeavors are on a lofty plane of constant advance and growth, is a matter of indifference to the Rebbe. The critical factors are the amount of effort expended and the magnitude of the obstacles overcome. Indeed, the Rebbe adds almost parenthetically, any thinking man can find some shortcoming in his effort to avoid evil.

Since the measure is the individual, the Rebbe asserts that the naturally endowed scholar who fails to exert himself in vigorous struggle is guilty of "unforgiveable sin . . . infinitely worse" than that of an ordinary person who is alienated from G-d and Torah and therefore does not restrain his lower impulses. But lest we erroneously infer from this that the Rebbe has different standards of conduct for different individuals, he insists that even a person who is passionate by nature and exposed more than others to temptations by reason of his occupation and environment, has no excuse whatsoever for sinning, for he, too, has been endowed with the capacity of restraining himself and controlling the lusts of his heart. Every man's mind is capable of controlling his heart's desires.

We have referred to a love of G-d that can overcome, or change the forces of habit and nature. This concept, that a natural trait is to be transformed, is perhaps one of the truly novel thoughts introduced by *Chabad.* It was articulated in a conversation between the Alter Rebbe (1745—1813) and his grandson, R. Menachem Mendel (1789—1866), and recounted by R. Menachem Mendel's great-grandson, the late Rebbe, R. Yoseph Yitzchak (1880—1950). "R. Menachem Mendel asked his grandfather, 'What is the essence (*inyan*) of *Chassidus*?' R. Menachem Mendel did not want a *definition* of *Chassidus,* for he was well aware that *Chassidus* is the inward aspect of Torah, the study of G-d. What he wanted to know was the ultimate *purpose* of *Chassidus.* The purpose of *Chassidus,* the grandfather replied, was to bring about a change in the *nature of one's personal traits."*

Chabad literature makes a special point of distinguishing between "effecting changes in natural *traits"* and "changing the *nature* of personal traits." "Effecting changes in natural traits" involves the extirpation of such undesirable characteristics as envy, violent temper or self-indulgence. These characteristics may be innate in man, but he is not their passive pawn. He has the ability to uproot them and to replace them with more admirable ones. This idea is not unique to *Chabad*; it was articulated at least as early as during the days of R. Saadia Gaon, some ten centuries ago. But *Chassidus,* as the Alter Rebbe explained to his grandson, has a goal that is much more ambitious and far-reaching. Even desirable traits, if they are merely innate, are not the summit of achievement.

At this point, let us digress briefly into a discourse by R. Yoseph Yitzchak, the immediate predecessor of the present Lubavitcher Rebbe. After Abraham had passed his supreme test of faith, having bound his own son Isaac to the altar as a sacrifice, G-d said to him, "Now I know that you are G-d-fearing." Now Abraham's characteristic way of serving G-d had always been based on love. Is not that kind of service, the Rebbe asks, superior to a service founded on fear? He then proceeds to answer his own question. Without a doubt, Abraham's love of G-d was sublime, and his love of man, too, was all-encompassing, extending even to the stranger and the undeserving. But Abraham did not acquire this quality through personal struggle; he had been born with it. To be sure, he was generous with his wealth and with his person, hospitable, kindly, and eager to share his material and spiritual possessions with the less favored. He made magnificent use of his natural talents. But they were only natural talents, not the fruits of Abraham's efforts. In fact, Abraham never considered himself to be an adequate servant of G-d, for he felt that all his service had been accomplished through the gifts with which G-d had endowed him, and not through his personal endeavors. It would not be blasphemous to suggest that perhaps G-d, too, was not "sure" whether Abraham's service was purely one of love because this was Abraham's very nature, or whether Abraham consciously felt that this was the proper way of serving G-d. Abraham was, after all, a free agent with a free will. Is the kindly person hospitable because he is kindly, or because G-d wills him to be so?

When Abraham, the epitome of kindliness, is prepared to act so cruelly toward his son, "his only son whom he loves," then he is acting contrary to his habit; he is suppressing his natural mercies, performing an act diametrically opposed to his innate nature. His motivation could only have been "fear of G-d," a new mode of Divine service, not usual or natural to him, but the result of deep personal conviction and hard personal struggle. Whether the service born of love is superior to the service based on awe or "fear" is irrelevant for our present purposes. Our concern is only whether the service is "natural" or whether it represents the fruit of effort, of *avodah*. This is the test of effort that Abraham had to pass when he readied his son for sacrifice.

Abraham added a new dimension to his service of G-d, for now, in addition to utilizing his natural trait of love in his relationship with G-d, he had succeeded in serving G-d also through the acquired quality of awe. Love and awe, each of these has its own appropriate function in the total service of G-d. His willingness to offer up his son as a sacrifice showed that even his "service of love" did not derive from his innate quality of good-heartedness, but from a conscious obedience to the Divine command, "Love your fellow" and "Love the L-rd your G-d."

Clearly, Abraham did not effect a change in his natural traits. His willingness to sacrifice his son to G-d did not entail an effort on the part of Abraham to extirpate an evil trait from his character. What it did involve was a change in the *nature* of his personal traits, from kindliness to sacrifice of his son. Whoever remains in the mold into which he was born—though his traits in themselves are beyond reproach—is simply preserving a set of good habits. Worship itself—when it is permitted to become a matter of routine—can become frigid, a product of habit, devoid of the intense desire to do the will of the Creator and to serve Him with gladness. There are situations when an individual who is kindly by nature must be capable of sternness, when the studious individual is called upon to develop the emotional aspects of his being, when the extrovert must put his inward qualities to use—this list can easily be extended. This, a change in the *nature* of one's personal traits, is the purpose of *Chassidus*—obviously a formidable challenge to anyone, no matter what his past achievements, as is made clear by the following *Chabad* explanation.

Moses is described as the "humblest of all men." Humility, as *Chabad* understands it, is not self-deprecation. Humility can exist simultaneously with full appreciation of one's own personal worth and even superiority over others. Moses' humility was expressed in his realization that his unusual qualities were not the products of his own effort, but gifts bestowed upon him by G-d and by family background and heredity. His father, Amram of the tribe of Levi, had been one of the "great men of his generation." Moses did not think it was for his own merit that G-d had revealed Himself to him so many times, first at the burning bush and them, most awesome of all, atop Mount Sinai. Had any individual out of the multitudes of Israel been given the opportunities so freely granted to him, Moses was convinced, this person would have accomplished far more than he, Moses, had done. This is the mark of true humility. Moses was fully aware that he towered above all his contemporaries in learning and in spirit, but he felt he deserved no special credit for that. It had all been given to him by the bounty of G-d. Only qualities attained by personal effort, Moses felt, were deserving of respect, and he, alas, had never exerted real effort.

It is a custom for *Chassidim* to go to their rebbe to obtain his blessing. The blessing might be for good health, for prosperity, or for whatever else the *Chassid* might need. But the *Chabad Chassid* particularly cherishes his Rebbe's blessing for success in his spiritual endeavors, in Torah study and in worship, in the development of his own soul.

A *Chassid* once asked R. Menachem Mendel to bless his grandson that he acquire a good memory in order to "remember whatever he sees and hears of the Rebbe and the *Chassidim,* and then he will be G-d .fearing as a matter of course."

"For more than fifty years now my grandfather, (R. Shneur Zalman of Liadi) my father-in-law (R. Dov Ber, R. Shneur Zalman's son) and I have labored that *Chassidim* should be G-d-fearing not as a matter of course but as a result of diligent labor," R. Menachem Mendel replied.

On Torah

based on Likutei Torah, Vayikra, p. 4.

Since man was made in the image of G-d, we may gain some insight into G-d by understanding man. Soul, which is the essence of man, possesses powers deriving from the *sephirot,* the attributes and powers of G-d. Though, of course, we must beware of anthropomorphizing G-d's attributes ("for," as Isaiah put it in 55:9, "My thoughts are not your thoughts"), we may say that the soul-powers of man and the attributes of G-d parallel each other.

"Soul" and "powers" are not synonymous. As the very definition of the term "essence" indicates, "soul" is irreducible, indivisible. Soul acts through its "powers" (intellectual and emotive) and its "garments" (thought, speech, and action). Thought, word, and deed—these are the instruments of the soul. Similarly, the *sephirot,* the "powers" of G-d, are the instruments through which He manifests Himself, be it as Judge, as Father, or as Warrior.

The initial, and highest, manifestation or power of the soul, and accordingly, the highest *sefira,* is *chochmah.* It is the initial spark of revelation, unshaped, seminal. It is not an independent entity, for it has not yet acquired substance and so may be fleeting, transitory. It is permeated with consciousness of its source. It is amorphous and hence in a state of relative nullity. The demarcation line between *chochmah* and soul is a delicate one, so much so that we are warned that "soul" and "powers" are not identical. Indeed, some do go so far as to equate this first power with the soul or to define G-d as Intellect. However, the Alter Rebbe

explained, the synonymity extends only to the manifestation of soul, or of G-d, not to the essence, i.e. not to the soul
itself or G-d Himself.

In any event, though soul transcends intellect, intellect
serves as its instrument. To the degree that we may speak
of the essence of soul being revealed, *chochmah* is its vehicle;
to the degree that we may speak of G-d's Essence being
revealed or apprehended, intellect (or more specifically,
intellect's origin-state, namely *chochmah*) is its vehicle. Soul
clothes itself in intellect. Soul thinks.

The Zohar describes the mitzvot as "organs of the King";
each *mitzvah* is an instrument or vessel for the Divine Light,
meaning the revelation of G-d. Torah, the *mitzvah* of the
mind, is the vessel for the Divine Wisdom, the instrument
through which the Divine Intellect acts and manifests itself.
(By extension, G-d's "emotions" or creative powers, for
example, are displayed through other instruments.) Wisdom is clothed in Torah. Let us repeat that *chochmah* is not
the essence of G-d or man, but essence is revealed through
chochmah. We now have the parallel between man and his
intellect, on the one hand, and G-d and the Divine Intellect, on the other.

The Divine Wisdom permeates its instrument, which is
the Torah. Man's mind in turn engages in the study of
Torah. The link is now established. G-d's Essence is clothed
in the attribute of *chochmah,* which in turn manifests itself
in the various teachings of Torah. Man's intellect is immersed in Torah, while his own soul employs and invests
intellect in this endeavor. Thus the essence of soul and the
essence of G-d are united through the instrumentality of
Torah, and can be so united only through Torah.

The Alter Rebbe brought this lofty experience within the
grasp of ordinary men when he observed that this union
may be perfectly valid, even if it is unconscious, with the
student being unaware of his bond with G-d. We must
remember that during study man's consciousness is entirely involved with the subject matter at hand, with the
effort to attain intellectual mastery of the material. In fact,

he may not be impervious to a touch of smugness when he has accomplished an intellectual feat—and this bit of ego smacks, however faintly, of arrogance. Still, his ultimate purpose is good; he studies Torah for Torah's sake; he thirsts for the teachings of G-d. His soul in its innermost recesses unites with G-d. If mortal man does not sense this union, his "soul above" * does. . .

Mortal intellect is limited—it can fully grasp only the mundane. It may know of the existence of the spiritual, but cannot conceive its nature and character.

These two degrees of knowledge are discussed at some length in *Chabad* literature, for the distinction helps define the capacities and limitations of the human, finite mind. The fact that we cannot comprehend or describe either G-d or the soul, for example, does not exclude them from intellectual consideration, nor should we denigrate whatever knowledge we do have of them. For instance, one might declare the existence of the Creator, and cite all sorts of relevant arguments and proofs for one's statement, but still not be able to describe the Creator at all. This is common in science, a scientist postulating the existence of a sub-atomic particle without being able to describe it at all. We may say that men can have knowledge of the Creator's "existence", but not of His "character" or "nature." In general, we may say that man's experience and knowledge is with the dimensional, which he is capable of mastering intellectually. Just because he cannot comprehend the supra-rational, the infinite, this does not mean that the infinite does not exist, nor does it imply that man cannot know of the existence of infinite. Naturally, as one grows intellectually, the scope of his knowledge of "character" will grow; he will be able to comprehend today that which eluded him yesterday.

Because of the distinction between the two classes of knowledge, there is a basic difference in the study of Tal-

---

*Briefly, only a portion of the soul is invested in the body; the major part is Above, "before G-d."

mud and *Kabbalah*. The subject matter of the Talmud is accessible to the mortal mind, for it deals with concrete objects and situations. In mastering the Talmud one thoroughly grasps the Divine Wisdom incorporated within it. In studying *Kabbalah,* on the other hand, one deals with terms and abstract concepts that defy comprehension. There is an intellectual barrier to comprehension, and the Divine Wisdom invested in *Kabbalah* remains beyond boundaries which man cannot cross.

It might be inferred that since there can be no true comprehension of *Kabbalah,* the study of *Kabbalah,* in contrast to that of *Mishna* and Talmud, involves an element of superficiality. However, the Rebbe cautioned, this is no reason looking down upon the study of *Kabbalah*. Intellect and comprehension have their place, and a supremely honored one it is, in the Torah scheme. But our Sages urge us to spend "one third of our time in Scripture study." The Rebbe explained that Scripture, as distinct from the Oral Torah, refers to the *word* of Torah as distinct from the *idea* of Torah. The indispensable criterion of Talmudic study is intellect; reciting the words of Talmud without knowing their meaning is a sheer waste of time. By contrast, the illiterate who recites the words of Scripture even though he does not understand them *does* perform a *mitzvah* of major proportions. The classic practice of "saying *Tehillim,*" reciting Psalms, is a case in point. Another might be the weekly review of the Torah portion with the Aramaic translation, *Onkelos.*

This aspect of Scripture is hardly limited to the illiterate; it is an innate aspect of Scripture. For this reason there are numerous Biblical verses which are beyond rational grasp but which we recite nevertheless, without our really knowing their sense. Maimonides, as noted in an earlier essay, declares that passages such as, "The sons of Ham were Cush and Mizraim . . ." (Gen. 10:6) or "The name of his wife was Mehitabel" (Gen. 36:39) are no less sacred than "I am the L-rd your G-d" (Exod. 20:2) or "Hear O Israel . . ." (Deut. 6:4). To be sure, the mortal mind does not perceive these two categories of Biblical verses as being on the same intellectual plane, but intellect does not exhaust their significance. All four passages emanate from the same Divine source, beyond the reach of man's mind.

The *Kabbalah,* the Rebbe explained, and also the *Aggadah* (the homiletical, narrative part of the Oral tradition), come under the generic heading of "Scripture." Their significance is not intellectual, for the mind is not the instrument designed to deal with them.

Given the seemingly obvious meaning and simplicity of the Biblical narrative, it is difficult to distinguish the profound Divine wisdom incorporated in the sacred text. The factual veracity of the narrative is not the full meaning of the "story." The mind can comprehend only the external, the simple meaning. According to the Zohar, laws are the "body" of Torah while narratives are called its "garb." Drawing analogies from sensory perceptions and utilizing Torah passages, the Rebbe said that laws must be "tasted," while narratives are "aromas," subtle, unpalpable, which can be detected even from a distance.

The characters and events mentioned in the Torah are particular and actual on one hand, and at the same time paradigms on another level of comprehension. *Kabbalah* and *Chassidus* constantly speak of the physical world as a manifestation or concretization of their spiritual parallels or sources. In this view "animal" and "angel," for example, are not antipodes. More than symbolic language is intended in Torah—it is reality on a variety of planes. Yet, though the true meaning of narratives may elude our minds, we should not consider them alien or inaccessible to us.

Torah is the link between man and G-d. This intermediary, as it were, has both revealed and hidden aspects which parallel the revealed and hidden aspects of the soul, and the revealed and hidden aspects of G-d. Through the Revealed Torah, *Mishna* and Talmud, which are within the grasp of man's understanding, the revealed aspects of man are united with the revealed aspects of G-d. Through

Scripture (which includes *Aggadah* and *Kabbalah*), i.e. the Hidden Torah, the hidden and inward aspects of soul are bound up with the Concealed aspects of G-d. *Halacha* study, the Rebbe declared citing *Avot deRabi Natan 29,* leads to wisdom for it can be grasped, but *Midrash* study, though not perfectly comprehended, leads to piety.

Glossary

Aggadah

non-legal portions of Talmud, especially interpretations of Biblical verses, history, anecdotes, moral exhortation, etc.

Ahavas Yisroel

Love of one's fellow Jew

Alter Rebbe

"Old" Rebbe; popular name for R. Schneur Zalman (1745—1813), founder of Chabad Chassidus, first Rebbe of the Lubavitcher

Ari

R. Yitzhak Luria, leading Kabbalist in Safed four centuries ago. Chabad is based largely on his works. "Ari" is an acronym for Our Master Reb Yitzhak and means "lion" in Hebrew.

avodah

labor; service; worship

Baal Shem Tov

"Master of the Good Name"; R. Israel (1698—1760), founder of the Chassidic movement

batel (bitul)

null (nullification); Ego, self-awareness, stands in the way of true avodah. Man is to "nullify" his ego through awareness of One higher than himself.

benoni

Tanya describes the tzaddik as the unusually sinless saint impervious to temptation, the rasha as the unrepentant sinner, and the benoni as faultless in deed, word and thought, but subject to temptation. The benoni controls himself by effort. The standard of the benoni, the Rebbe insists, is the "measure of all men."

binah

In Chabad usage there are three steps in intellectual achievement: chochmah (wisdom) is creative, original, seminal; binah (understanding) is developmental; daat (knowledge) brings application and conclusion.

bracha	blessing
Chabad	acronym for chochmah, binah, daat (see "binah"); name of R. Schneur Zalman's school within the Chassidic movement
Chassidus	Movement emphasizing joy in serving G-d, enthusiastic worship and love of one another regardless of merit; see "Baal Shem Tov"
chessed	"kindness"; After the three steps of intellect (see "binah"), application follows: a legal decision for example or an emotion consonant with the thought. Contemplation of G-d's bounty, for instance, might arouse an emotion of love, while pondering His Majesty may arouse awe or fear. The first category of emotions— positive, attraction, love—is called chessed, "kindness," while the second—withdrawing, withholding, awe, fear—comes under gevurah, "strength," severity.
chinuch	education, training, dedication
chochmah	see "binah"
chok	(chukim, pl.) transrational mitzvot
Chumash	Pentateuch, Five Books of Moses (Genesis through Deuteronomy)
Codes	works presenting verdicts in Talmudic law
Commentaries	elucidations of Talmudic texts, the most famous probably being Rashi
Concealed Torah	One plane of Torah is accessible to the intellect, particularly the legal plane. The "inner" or esoteric plane is not readily grasped. Kabbalah, the most famous work being the Zohar, is an example of this genre. Chassidus, liberally using Kabbalah, is another example.
daat	see "binah"
daven	worship; "Davening" plays a major role in Chassidus and Chabad.

GLOSSARY

edot	"testimonial" mitzvot (matzah on Pesach for example)
emunah	faith
Gemara	exposition of Mishna; together they are often called Talmud; contains halacha and aggadah
gevurah	see "chessed"
halacha	"law"; based on Biblical sources developed in Talmud and definitively stated in the Codes
Kabbalah	see "Concealed Torah"
licht-bentchen	candle-lighting on Sabbath and festival eve
Lubavitch	town in White Russia where Chabad Rebbes lived for 102 years from 1813. "Lubavitcher" and "Chabad" are used interchangeably.
Maariv	evening davening
Midrash	Aggadic literature
Mincha	afternoon davening
Mishna	post-Biblical Torah law
Misnaged	"Opponent" of Chassidus
Mitzvah (Mitzvot pl.)	Torah commandments
Mussar	moral-ethical literature; renewed impetus given in 1800's to Mussar study and values by R. Israel Salanter in Lithuania
neshama	soul
shtetl	east European village
Talmud	see "Gemara"
tefillin	boxes placed on arm and head with leather straps, contain parchment scrolls with Biblical passages including Sh'ma; worn by males past Bar Mitzvah during weekday morning davening
tzaddik	righteous; see "benoni"

yarmulka   skull-cap; worn as a reminder of One higher
                            than man

Yiddishkeit   Jewishness (not a matter of language)

For the reader unfamiliar with names of Chassidic leaders:
  R. Israel Baal Shem Tov (1698-1760), founder of the Chassidic move-
    ment
  R.Dovber, Maggid of Mezritch (?-1772), his successor
  R.Schneur Zalman (1745-1813), founder of Chabad, the "Alter Rebbe"
  R. Dovber (1773-1827)
  R. Menachem Mendel (1789-1866), author of *Tzemach Tzedek*
  R. Shmuel (1834-1882)
  R. Sholom Dovber (1860-1920)
  R. Yoseph Yitzhak (1880-1950)
  R. Menachem Mendel Schneerson, the Lubavitcher Rebbe